Minds More Awake

MINDS MORE AWAKE

The Vision of Charlotte Mason

by

Anne E. White

ISBN-13 978-0-9947977-0-4

CONTENTS

Acknowledgements / Thanks

Thank you to Susan Schaeffer Macaulay for writing For the Children's Sake, the book which introduced so many of us to the work of Charlotte Mason.

The AmblesideOnline Advisory: Donna-Jean Breckenridge, Lynn Bruce, Wendi Capehart, Karen Glass, Leslie Noelani Laurio. Thank you especially to Karen and to Melanie Rudd for proofreading and for many helpful suggestions.

The AmblesideOnline Auxiliary: Naomi Goegan, Melisa Hills, Phyllis Hunsucker, Kathy Livingston, Lani Siciliano, Amy Tuttle, Brandy Vencel, Jeanne Webb.

The local Charlotte Mason Moms: thanks for all the great discussions!

Thank you to Kelly Gibbons, my co-moderator for ten years on CMCanada.

Douglas White, for technical advice.

Most of all, thank you to my family: Bryan, Josanne, Audrey, and Lydia, for photography, graphics, tech talk, and much more.

*"All we find may be old knowledge, and is most
likely already recorded in books;
but for us, it is new, our own discovery,
our personal knowledge,
a little bit of the world's real work
which we have attempted and done."
Charlotte Mason*

Beginnings

Twenty years ago, I discovered Charlotte Mason in a church library cart.

Our church congregation met in a hall at a nearby college. We had a small storage area, but no permanent arrangements for worship or teaching. The sound team arrived early each Sunday to lay out cords and hook up microphones. Babies were cared for in a lounge, with a couple of folding playpens and a bin of toys. And our library was housed in a cart that we rolled out at the end of each service.

One Sunday, I picked up a copy of Susan Schaeffer Macaulay's *For the Children's Sake.*[1] When I asked around later, nobody seemed to know where it came from or who had put it in the library. Anyway, I signed it out and put it in the diaper bag along with my toddler's cereal snack. I didn't know that reading it would change not only my life, but, indirectly, the lives of others.

I read about two little girls who were bored and unhappy at school, until their parents found them a place to learn that spoke to their hearts and spirits as well as their minds. I read about children looking at paintings, exploring outdoors, and reading real books. Suddenly I made the connection: Francis Schaeffer? Not that guy with the beard in those films about babies that our parents took us to in the 1970's?[2] Yes, the same. And these girls were his grandchildren. Well, then.

Our church had gone through some growing pains, and at that time it was so small that there was only one Sunday school class, for school-aged children. I had a very active and verbal two-year-old who proclaimed herself too big for the baby lounge, and there were two or three others of about the same age. I asked the elders if I could have a class time for them, during the last half of the service. They encouraged me to go ahead, and buy whatever toys or supplies we needed. But what I really wanted to do was try out Charlotte Mason.

We had a music practice room, not a children's classroom, and sometimes we had to vacuum the floor or push tables around before the little ones could use it; but that was all right, Charlotte Mason and

Susan said environments didn't have to be perfect. We brought crayons, a cassette player, and couch cushions for the floor. We bought a big tub of used plastic bricks, and stuck pictures up on the wall. Whenever we could, we took the children for "nature walks" by the creek right outside the door. We told stories with little plastic people, and acted things out together. The children went home and talked about the ducks and the Bible people. For the next two years, that's what four preschoolers and I (and their involved and supportive parents) did on Sundays.

A few years later, we were attending a different church, and I had another preschooler. Again, there was nothing much for that age group, and I offered to start a class. But these new children seemed...not more immature, so much as just bored (unless there was food involved). I took them outside looking for pine cones. We pretended we were on Noah's Ark. Almost everything fell flat. The parents dropped their children off at the door, but never asked to come in or to see what we were doing. After trying to make the class work for awhile, I gave it up, and nobody seemed to care. What made the difference? From the children, I got a sense of overload (at that age!). The class was just one more place, one more stop-off in an already busy week. But that wasn't what I wanted for our own family. Our children needed to have time in their lives for wonder.

I went back and re-read *For the Children's Sake,* and Susan's (then) brand-new book, *For the Family's Sake: The Value of Home in Everyone's Life.*[3] And Charlotte Mason's *Home Education Series,* first borrowed from our homeschool group's library, and then my own set that we found at a used bookstore.[4] (Like the church library book, its appearance just then seemed to be, perhaps, a little hello-wave from God.) Coincidentally, we were beginning our first year of seriously trying to use Charlotte Mason's methods in our family's homeschool. More coincidentally: the online curriculum project that became AmblesideOnline[5] went live later that fall, and we joined in.

Each of the families from our first class ended up homeschooling their children (they did not all plan to at the time), and we have all stayed in touch. I still like to think that the two years we met in that improvised classroom helped to stir all of our hearts "for the children's sake."

Chapter 1: Charlotte Mason and a Slow Cooker

> As things are we shall have to see to it that
> everybody gets fed; but our hope is that
> henceforth we shall bring up our young
> people with self-sustaining minds, as well as
> self-sustaining bodies, by a due ordering of
> the process of education. We hope so to
> awaken and direct mind hunger that every
> man's mind will look after itself. (*Philosophy of
> Education*) [1]

I have always loved putting bits and pieces together and rescuing leftovers, to the occasional horror of my children. I'm not over-confident in my kitchen abilities; I season according to the recipe or by guess. I have never been much of a meat cooker (I ask my husband if I'm not sure), and there are many things that I have never cooked and never will. A professional chef I am not.

But as Peg Bracken said half a century ago, you don't always need fancy recipes, and sometimes you're better off without them.

> "Worst of all, there are the big fat
> cookbooks that tell you everything about

everything. For one thing, they contain too
many recipes. Just look at all the things you
can do with a chop, and aren't about to!
What you want is just one little old
dependable thing you can do with a chop
besides broil it, that's all."[2]

Well, we are not broiled-chop people, but you get the drift. My own "little old dependable thing" has usually been putting whatever-it-is on a layer of sauerkraut, and turning on the slow cooker. Like Peg Bracken, I am happy to find a good recipe or two, but mostly I cook on principles gained from experience, which have often saved me from wasting my time on *bad* recipes. It's when I ignore my instincts, and the laws of food nature, that dinner turns out badly. "Too much liquid for a slow cooker recipe, that's going to be a mess," I thought; and sure enough, I had to doctor the too-soupy chili with extra cans of beans.

My favourite cookbook authors describe good cooking as a generous art, both in the fellowship of the meal and in the sharing of techniques, recipes, ideas. When I was first married, I got involved with programs at a community centre. One of our groups was a cooking and nutrition class, neighbours teaching neighbours. A Japanese executive's wife stir-fried beef with spinach and sesame seeds. An Eastern European woman made an apple dessert. The German-born nutrition worker brought in things that interested her, like spelt and muesli. I learned a lot just by watching how other people functioned in the kitchen.

Which brings us back to where we started: one of the problems today is that many people just don't have that experience and so don't have confidence, or they have been told that cooking is mysterious, and time-consuming. But is it such a mystery that when you put tomatoes, beans and chili powder into the slow cooker (with the *right* amount of liquid), and let it simmer for the afternoon, it turns into dinner? Maybe you add meat or hot peppers, use a different kind of beans, but that's fine too. There is a principle at work here, and, properly applied and barring power blackouts, it should work for everyone.

Charlotte Mason was a teacher of teachers, a writer, and a

generous inspirer. She taught by principles, method, and natural laws, and hesitated to give too many specific directions in case her work turned into a "big fat cookbook."[3] She knew that people hoped for the promise of the latest foolproof parenting and teaching system, no matter what the cost; but she had no interest in marketing the educational equivalent of an overloaded sport vehicle. Nonetheless, she did produce six volumes on education—her links in the chain of the classical tradition.

Back to the Beginning

Sometimes we get into a thinking rut and can't imagine a simpler way of doing what has always been complicated. I read once about an older woman who streamlined her housework with the help of Don Aslett's cleaning books.[4] What used to take her most of the day now required only an hour or two, and she suddenly had much more free time to do other things. Now she had a new problem: her husband thought she was lazy because she wasn't spending hours cleaning the floors and the toilets. But she had discovered what worked, and she wasn't going back.

In the same way that a car is, more or less, an engine in a box attached to a set of wheels, human beings are constructed in certain predictable ways. We have the same basic desires; our memories mostly work the same way; we are made to have certain natural relationships with each other, with the world around us, and with a Creator. When we understand who we are and how we work, we start to get right ideas about how we acquire and use knowledge. We can use those ideas to teach children, our own or other people's; we can also use them to examine larger life issues. Are we making our world a better home for human beings, or are we fighting our own natures? Are we educating for compassion, or for a global workforce?

This form of education—whether we call it Charlotte Mason, PNEU methods, or holistic-synthetic-organic learning—is not a fad. It is not just another option on the curriculum table. It is a conviction, and an active response to that conviction. Do we believe that children really want to know? Then, said Charlotte Mason, we will teach from and with that belief, "and, knowing this, our teaching becomes buoyant with the courage of our convictions."[5]

At the end of this book is a list of Charlotte Mason's twenty principles of education. Over many years, many people have explored, broken down, and written about this list. We can think of it as the Beatitudes of Mason, or the Twenty Commandments. However, just because something has been much discussed doesn't mean it's not worth looking at again; or that it's not still misunderstood or misapplied.

For instance, Charlotte Mason's second principle, "[Children] are not born bad but with possibilities for good and evil," is enough to raise quite a lot of homeschooling and religious hackles. *"What do you mean, children are not born bad?" "What about our sinful natures?" "I'm going back to classical."*

> [Children are born] with tendencies,
> dispositions, towards good and towards evil,
> and also with a curious intuitive knowledge
> as to which is good and which is evil. Here
> we have the work of education indicated.[6]

> In every child there are tendencies to
> greediness, restlessness, sloth, impurity, any
> one of which by allowance may ruin the
> child and the man that he will be.[7]

I am convinced that Charlotte Mason did not intend to set off a theological storm here. The point she was making was about the possibilities for good, for self-management over negative tendencies, for nobility and heroism, in every single child; and her belief that those possibilities could be encouraged by good teaching. In fact, that was the ultimate aim of her educational methods: to produce character, instruct a conscience, develop a will. The goal was to build up an adult human being who could manage not only him or herself, but also a family, a business, school, church, or town, maybe even a country; and serve God over all.

> We cannot make a child "good"; but, in this
> way, we can lay paths for the good life in the
> very substance of his brain...[8]

Charlotte Mason pointed out that, by her time, church teaching had moved from a focus mainly on personal salvation to a larger outlook that showed greater social concern. She did not mean that salvation was unimportant, but that chronic obsession with one's own sinful nature was missing God's grace, and that it was particularly pernicious to inflict this self-focused attitude on children. Children, she wrote (perhaps thinking of herself as a child), can be miserably aware of their own sinful natures without being continually reminded of them.

Just as views on the state of children's souls had shifted, educational attitudes were also changing. It had been thought that the upper classes were born not only morally better but also more intelligent; but that belief was now in question. Scientists had discovered that what we learn is physically imprinted in our brains, meaning that upper-class craniums held identical matter to lower-class ones. If brains showed the physical effects of education, then it didn't matter what you were born with or what your early experiences were; anyone could learn, change and grow. Mason called this discovery of the physiological basis of habit formation "the charter of our liberties," meaning that no individual was a slave to his genealogy. She got excited when she thought about the educational possibilities that could go beyond just one child or one group, to something that could rock the world.

This also showed, more clearly than ever, what an awe-inspiring task it is to be a parent. Mason thought that the philosopher Rousseau's most important contribution was simply pointing out that bringing up children is an important job.[9] Developmental psychologists never stop telling us how awake and receptive young children's minds are. A mother or father sows the first seeds of attitudes, personal habits, relationships, disposition. Charlotte Mason trained governesses and teachers, but she warned parents about entrusting their children too much to even well-meaning others. Children may not come with owners' manuals, but they do come with attached responsibilities.

However, there are limits even for parents. Children are not balls of clay to be moulded, or bonsai trees to be clipped and trimmed. "Education" may come from words that mean, "to draw out," but Mason preferred the term "bringing up" as not sounding so much like a pair of parental forceps.[10]

Another image she liked was "building backbone," which implies inner growth and strength. If parents allow children to sprawl physically, they will not have the habit of good posture. Children allowed to sprawl intellectually will develop sloppy thinking habits. A character in a novel is described with the words, "He had never learned to make himself do the thing he would." It was always "what I like" instead of "what I ought." There was no power of self-direction, no force of character.

If we want children to grow up with power, force, backbone, they must begin early to know that they *can* and *ought*; this is education. Even small children *can* and *ought* to be in training to be obedient, self-controlled, generous, patient, kind, Godly, and loving. If we teach those habits gradually but early, through example and through words, children begin to recognize that they have the strength to "make themselves do the things they would."

Why is Charlotte Mason like a slow cooker?

Because you have to leave the lid on, and trust the process. If the power is flowing, dinner will cook itself.

Chapter 2:   Start Here (The Way of the Will)

> [A person of will has] the power to project
> himself beyond himself and shape his life
> upon a purpose. (*Ourselves*) [1]

> It takes the whole man to will, and a man
> wills wisely, justly, and strongly in
> proportion as all his powers are in training
> and under instruction. (*Ourselves*) [2]

My first experience with Charlotte Mason's own books was a common one. I started reading at the beginning of *Home Education*, all nannies and nurseries, and got stuck at wool clothing and beef tea. Luckily, I made it beyond the first chapters and soon found myself in the more congenial territory of early math and walks in the woods. *Pilgrim's Progress*, I knew well; Plutarch, I didn't, but that would come eventually.[3]

I don't remember catching the idea, right away, that so much of what happens in a Charlotte Mason education is connected with the rather mystical Way of the Will. Yes, it is there in the basic principles at the front of every volume; and once you start looking for the Will in her books, it's all over the place. But somehow my mental diagram put the Way of the Will and the Way of the Reason at about the same point where they're discussed in *Philosophy of Education*: on page 128. Kind of like the Indo-Malaya section of the Toronto Zoo: if you get that far, it's interesting, but optional. If you miss seeing the Reticulated Python, no great loss.

However, I've become convinced that the Way of the Will is, in fact, the Start Here point on Charlotte Mason's map. It is Christian's Wicket Gate in *Pilgrim's Progress*, Lucy's Lamp Post in Narnia. We need to work through it to understand Mason's approach to literature, science, even beef tea.

Tracing Out the Problem

A friend's telephone line has been on the fritz.

She described the problem to my husband, who used to work for the phone company, and asked him if he had any idea what the reason could be.

"I know exactly what's wrong," he told her. "When you had that electrical work done last fall and they dug around on your street, the insulation on the cable was damaged somewhere. Now all the moisture from the spring thaw has gotten in there and it's shorting out."

"But what do we do about it?" she asked. "They've sent two technicians already and it's still not fixed."

"That's because some of the younger techs are trained to look at very specific problems, but they're not as good at putting the whole picture together. Probably what will happen next is that they'll send out a senior guy who will test the line, find out where the problem is, and fix it."

She nodded and then asked, "How did you figure out the answer, just like that?"

"Well, I think about what the problem isn't," said my husband, "and that narrows it down to what it is."

Young teacher Charlotte Mason also had a problem, back in the late nineteenth century. She noticed that, even with her not-too-challenging, middle-class students, something was missing.

> The faults they had, they kept; the virtues
> they had were exercised just as fitfully as
> before. The good, meek little girl still told
> fibs. The bright, generous child was

> incurably idle. In lessons it was the same
> thing; the dawdling child went on dawdling,
> the dull child became no brighter. It was
> very disappointing.[4]

So, like a good telephone technician, Charlotte Mason decided to trace the trouble to its source. She observed that the children's natural tendencies did not seem to respond with long-term results to outward correction (such as typical schoolroom punishments). Therefore, the "trouble," as the technician would say, was an inside rather than an outside problem.

And since it seemed impossible for children's natures, like telephone lines, to repair themselves, the best solution (and the one that our friend hopes will not have to happen) was to lay down new lines.

> But habit, to be the lever to lift the child,
> must work contrary to nature, or at any rate,
> independently of her...it rests with parents
> and teachers to lay down lines of habit on
> which the life of the child may run
> henceforth with little jolting or miscarriage,
> and may advance in the right direction with
> the minimum of effort.[5]

In *Home Education*, Charlotte Mason went on to talk about many sorts of habits, from shutting doors to truthfulness. She pointed out that since we are all, admittedly, creatures of habit, the best thing that parents can do for their children is to give them habits of "order, propriety, and virtue." There is nothing sacrilegious or arrogant about training children out of habits that they might have to repent of later as besetting sins.

> [Parents or teachers are] only to initiate [the
> ideas]; no more is permitted to them; but
> from this initiation will result the habits of
> thought and feeling which govern the
> man—his character, that is to say.[6]

19

The Way of the Will

When Charlotte Mason wrote about her early days of teaching, she said they were often frustrating because each year the children seemed able to do harder schoolwork, but they did not grow, either in moral power, or in having minds that were increasingly awake to the love of knowledge. The habits that needed to be established early were not just about courtesy and hygiene; they included attentiveness, rapid mental effort, and imagination. (Those are good things to learn early if you want to solve telecommunication problems.)

When we teach strong habits of body and mind, we give our children leisure—freedom from anxiety. They don't have to stress about whether they are going to work attentively at their lessons or dawdle or get distracted; whether they are going to tell the truth or not. Adults have stronger wills; we can tell ourselves to get back to work after a break, or make a decision that puts others first. Children don't have that power fully developed yet, so it is important to begin with the discipline of habit, then work on developing the Will gradually.

Charlotte Mason said a person acting with Will should be chivalrous, that is, demonstrating noble and knightly qualities such as courage, honour, and care for the weak. David V. Hicks calls these principles "norms and nobility."[7] Martha C. Nussbaum calls them our "narrative imagination."[8] But this idea of the Will as part of the soul (along with the intellect or reason, and the memory or conscience) goes back even further than Charlotte Mason. The philosopher Comenius wrote,

> In order, then, that these faculties may
> rightly fulfil their offices, it is necessary that
> they be furnished with such things as may
> illumine the intellect, direct the will, and
> stimulate the conscience, so that the intellect
> may be acute and penetrating, the will may
> choose without error, and the conscience
> may greedily refer all things to God.[9]

The Will is a sentry, protecting the castle or the town. It chooses which ideas we will allow through the gate, and, because ideas become actions, decides what we are going to do about them. We may make the mistake of thinking that we do not have the power to choose our thoughts; how many times have we been plagued with a nasty memory or anxiety that won't go away? However, the Will (if we imagine Will as a person) can be a very effective head of security. Rogue thoughts that have snuck in already are another matter, harder to deal with, but those still trying to gain entrance are the Will's business. He can buzz Conscience and other backups for advice, but the decision is his.

The Principle of the Thing

> Is there anything more attractive than the
> dignity and peacefulness of a steady will and
> a mind at one with itself? (Mrs.
> Ward, *Parents' Review*) [10]

The Way of the Will is principle-driven. It may have executive power, but it makes its decisions based on guidelines that have been handed to it. But where do those principles come from? If you don't have principles of your own, someone else will happily hand you some, but that is not a healthy way to function.

That does not mean that we accept every idea that comes along, or that we are afraid to voice our opinions; it does mean that we need well-developed principles to support the Will. And the opposite is true: using Will shapes our character. Acting with courage, generosity, and nobility shows that you are acting with Will, although Will itself isn't a conscience, isn't concerned with morality. The conscience can be tainted, but Will can still be doing an excellent job doing what it's supposed to be doing, like the dependable bodyguard of an evil tyrant.

But Will must have an object outside of itself, just as a guard is not there to protect himself. It cannot be focused on you, even for good ends such as personal health or salvation, because then it stops being Will. You can be operating with Will when your ultimate intent is to benefit a cause or a country, or to serve God, or to protect just one other person. And you can be missing out on Will if you're doing good deeds from selfish motives.

Applying the Way of the Will with Younger Students

My first office job was through a temporary employment agency, one summer during university. The agency was so impressed with my typing and spelling that they sent me out to a store where the office secretary would soon be leaving on vacation. In other words, I was going to be a solo act, and I found out quickly that I wasn't even close to being ready. I mixed up invoices, hung up on people accidentally, and couldn't keep the names of the salespeople straight (it was a family business and they all seemed to have the same last name). I lasted there about two days.

I had another temp job where the employer asked me if I could use a word processing machine made by a company better known for its cameras. His secretary went out for lunch, phoned to say she was never coming back, and nobody knew how to access her files. Strangely enough, I figured that one out, and ended up staying for a couple of weeks until they hired another secretary.

Sometimes you can learn things on the job. Other times you had better not even try without some training. But when it comes to training children in habits and developing their Wills, how do you know how much, what and when? Why can't the schedule come in one of those little cram-course pamphlets ("XYZ Word Processing in Four EZ Lessons") that the temp agency used to supply us with?

Recently I heard a Charlotte Mason talk that pointed out the impossibility of always matching up nature books we are reading to the world around us.[11] Sometimes the book comes before the real-life experience, and sometimes it is a follow-up. (In the case of a book about space travel, it may never be experienced firsthand!) My children enjoyed the vivid descriptions of water creatures in *The Pond on My Windowsill: the story of a freshwater aquarium*, by Christopher Reynolds, although we had no aquarium.[12] In the same way, we can begin to build up noble principles and teach the importance of choosing, long before children are required to deal with serious decisions themselves.

In her *Parents' Review* article on Plutarch, Miss Ambler describes some of the qualities she sees there:

> Again, a few pages further on in the same
> "Life," we have the idea of self-control, self-

victory. And, here again, there is no
ostentatious pointing of a moral...Again, the
idea of self-control, and also ideas of
forgiveness, justice, and humility in times of
prosperity, are presented in a passage from
the "Life of Dion."[13]

So also in books for younger children, we look for examples of
forgiveness, self-control and so on—without "ostentatious pointing
of a moral." We let them see consequences, but also chivalry and
grace extended to others, which are often lacking in didactic
(moralistic) stories. In *The Tale of Jemima Puddle-Duck*, it is easy to see
how Jemima's silly behaviour leads to her entrapment by a fox; but it
is also worth noting that Rex the collie dog chases the fox away and
saves her from becoming dinner.[14] A child hearing the story may
notice that point, or may focus only on Jemima. We might comment
that Rex was clever or that he acted like a good friend, but we do not
turn Beatrix Potter into a Sunday school lesson.

The Limits of Teachers

Children may not be able to fully use their wills yet, but that does not
give us authority to manipulate or damage those wills—exactly the
opposite. When Charlotte Mason said,

His will is the safeguard of a man against the
unlawful intrusion of other persons,

that meant "keep out, this means you."[15] Yes, there is authority
and obedience; there is the habit of diligence and attentiveness in the
classroom. However, Charlotte Mason's fourth principle gives us an
automatic limit on what and how we teach. If children are born
persons, then we may not encroach on something that is uniquely
theirs: their personhood, and a certain right that goes along with
personhood, the right to develop Will to the fullest extent possible.
She pointed out that, on a practical level, parents and teachers must
not do for a child what he is quite capable of doing, for instance,
reading something aloud that he would be better off reading to
himself. This applies also to the child's intellectual and moral life, not
to mention spiritual (theological).

We can't learn for a child. We are not to think for him. And we are not to rob him of any opportunity that he has to put his own real effort, personal power, into moral action, whether that is remembering to close the door or keep his temper in check. The more practice he gets, the more those muscles will develop—or not. He needs to work on saying yes or no to "initial ideas." Taking time to help. Standing up for someone weaker. Being brave instead of complaining.

One of Charlotte Mason's favourite hymns says:

> The trivial round, the common task
> Will furnish all we ought to ask.
> Room to deny ourselves; a road
> To bring us daily nearer God. [16]

Charlotte Mason reminded us that we aim more at true character, which influences conduct, than at good conduct without true character. Yes, one of our goals as teachers is to instil good habits, like diligence, through example (real-life and literary) and through an environment that encourages success. We definitely want to see work well done, harmony between siblings, clean hands! It is true that children who get their work done quickly and keep their rooms spotless may be doing those things only to please us, or for other less-than-worthy reasons. Still, the small daily chores and habits are pieces that help to build character. Diligence in copywork may not be everything, but it is something.

Applying the Way of the Will with Older Students

> "I am, I can, I ought, I will." (Charlotte Mason's motto for students)

> Shall we live this aimless, drifting life, or shall we take upon us the responsibility of our lives, and will as we go? (*Ourselves*) [17]

Last winter my daughter went to a thrift store, which was having a half-price sale and was quite busy. In the next changing room there was some drama going on between a young girl and a mother. The mother didn't like what the daughter was choosing; the daughter didn't like what the mother was suggesting. The mother kept bringing skinny jeans and trendy clothes, the daughter wanted more casual sweaters. The mother said, "You're too fat to get into these clothes anyway. You should lay off the Christmas cookies." (The girl did not appear to be overweight.)

We obviously don't want to act like that woman, for quite a few reasons. But particularly in the teaching of Will, she gets an F.

Training the Will does not mean teachers laying down meaningless assignments (especially under the rationale that hard work builds character). It does not mean parents always telling children what to wear or buy. This is what I think it means: imparting a sense of who they are, what they're doing, and why they're doing it. A sense of *amming*, and *canning*, and *oughting*, and *willing*.

Shall we allow our children to take upon themselves the responsibility of their lives, and will as they go? Will we allow them to learn to use their reason, to choose, to make decisions without regret?

> 13 Till we all come in the unity of the faith,
> and of the knowledge of the Son of God,
> unto a perfect man, unto the measure of the
> stature of the fulness of Christ:
> 14 That we henceforth be no more children,
> tossed to and fro, and carried about with
> every wind of doctrine, by the sleight of
> men, and cunning craftiness, whereby they
> lie in wait to deceive;
> 15 But speaking the truth in love, may grow
> up into him in all things, which is the head,
> even Christ... Ephesians 4:13-15, KJV

Applying the Way of the Will with Adults

> It is the business of education to find some
> way of supplementing that weakness of will
> which is the bane of most of us as well as of
> the children. (*Home Education*) [18]

Living by our principles implies that there is meaning and order in the world; that our decisions and choices matter and make a difference. It means that we belong to our values, and that we are our values, to some extent. It is the opposite of alienation and meaninglessness. We know that we matter, that we belong, and that we can form relationships with things in the world, with other humans, and with God.

Therefore, we make real decisions, realizing that when we choose between things, we are choosing between ideas. A simple example might be wondering whether to buy discount-store clothing made in overseas factories. You want to buy a t-shirt for your child; is it better to protest exploitation of workers by buying only thrift store or "fair trade" clothing? Buying fabric and sewing it yourself? (Where does the fabric come from?) Buying the cheaper t-shirt so the factory doesn't close and the employees lose their jobs altogether? Buying the cheaper one as a protest-in-reverse against being made to pay several times as much for a "fairly traded" product; or because that's just how much money you have? Or buying the cheaper shirt and donating the difference to charity? This is suddenly not so simple.

What did Charlotte Mason say to do if you're feeling overwhelmed by the options, other than just asking your best friend for an opinion or checking out popular answers online? Give your brain a break, at least briefly. Go and think about something else for a while. Then come back. Look at your values, and consider how your choices might affect other people. What is it you "want?"—that is, not just "allow" or "want," as in "That pink shirt would be so cute on her," but Will, as in, "I have the opportunity to make a choice here."

One final point: this is how grownup wills are supposed to operate. Children should stay in the beginning stages of Will for as long as it takes them; and it might take a long time. Little children, according to Charlotte Mason, are not ready to depend on Will at all; they need training in habit first. It wears them (or anyone) out to have to choose every action every time, deciding whether they will wash their hands, feed the pet, listen to their parents. They might act "wilfully," but they don't act with a Will, and they shouldn't be punished for their inability to function beyond their normal development. Sometimes a good habit is a better default.

Lost Treasures of Charlotte Mason, #1

Philosophy of Education, Chapter IV, "Authority and Docility"

Part One

If there was a way to make sure a chapter would stay lost, it would be to title it "Authority and Docility." Docility sounds like exactly what we don't need more of, a lot of mindless sheep going where they're led.

However, that's not exactly what Charlotte Mason meant by docility. She began by questioning the idea that "obedience, voluntary or involuntary, is of the nature of slavishness." Is bowing to any kind of authority necessarily a bad thing?

> [Properly used] authority is, on the contrary,
> the condition without which liberty does not
> exist...

Say I am the teacher in a classroom. If the students accept my authority, not because I am superhuman, but because I am in a position of responsibility, then things will go smoothly and we can put all our attention on learning together; there will probably be few discipline problems. It's sometimes said that children should think that they can do anything they want, because we don't want to damage their little psyches, because we are under the impression that this is giving them freedom, or just because we want them to like us more. But—this is what matters—in such an environment, they are not being allowed to develop the *habit* or *power* of obedience. Something they should own is being taken from them. They are not respected enough to be given the right to choose; "self-authority" is a sham.

What typically happens is that misbehaviour gets out of hand, and the Big Person who, up until now, has pretended *not* to be in authority, comes down suddenly and harshly, like a parent who has ignored the squabbling in the back seat but then suddenly erupts. This is not authority. This is, equally, not docility.

> Docility implies equality...probably the quite
> delightful pursuit of knowledge affords the
> only intrinsic liberty for both teacher and
> taught.

When I am on a team of people volunteering to cook a church supper, we are all working towards the same end, getting the food and dishes on the tables at the right time and according to health-department rules. There is usually someone in charge whose authority we agree to follow so that the thing gets done. If she asks someone to mop the floor, it's not because she just likes to give orders, it's because that's what needs to be done then. All this is recognized without having to discuss it, because we are adults and hopefully we have gotten our psyches in sufficient order to handle a request to mop the floor. Docility balanced with rightful authority is "ordered freedom." It is no longer "you against me"; it is co-operation for the end that we both desire.

But to pretend to children that all is freedom, all is play, and that nobody will ever ask them to do anything they don't like to do: that is the lie. To allow children to whine or sulk for what they want so that the parent will eventually cave in, because all decisions are arbitrary, is also a lie. To believe that children must be entertained *before* they can pay attention, because they are not capable of training themselves to attend otherwise—that is the worst lie of all.

> In this way of learning the child comes to
> his own; he makes use of the authority
> which is in him in its highest function as a
> self-commanding, self-compelling power.

Children *are* intelligent. They *can* use their own power to choose to do what they *ought*. And if they know they *ought*, they *will*.

Part Two

Charlotte Mason gave a warning here that sounds unusual for her: that at times "even the Shakespearian drama... [or] poetry, even the most musical and emotional" may not have educational priority, or, at least, it cannot be all that we teach. Those who have used Charlotte Mason's methods for some time may feel that although they have had to work hard to put the "lovely extras"—poetry, music, handicrafts, nature walks—into the curriculum, they now enjoy them so much that those things could pretty much *be* the curriculum. We may get to a point (though we wouldn't have believed it) where Shakespeare is so familiar, almost easy, for our children, that we use it to justify less time spent on non-poetic studies. As a friend in another province was told by a homeschooling supervisor, Shakespeare can't be included in a fourth grader's curriculum because fourth graders don't read Shakespeare, it's too hard; so if a fourth grader is reading Shakespeare, he must be doing it just for fun, and it doesn't count.

But the world is a big, complex place, and children are not fully nourished on cookies, even English chocolate biscuits. Down to business, said Charlotte Mason: build up

> ...relations with places far and near, with the
> wide universe, with the past of history, with
> the social economics of the present, with the
> earth they live on and all its delightful
> progeny of beast and bird, plant and tree;
> with the sweet human affinities they entered
> into at birth; with their own country and
> other countries, and, above all, with that
> most sublime of human relationships—their
> relation to God.

The curriculum, she repeated, must be generous and wide: we need to build up our relationships with beasts and birds, plants and trees, geography, history, and even the global economy. In the first of his *Uncle Eric* books, Richard J. Maybury says that we should learn to see the world through four models: business, economic, legal, and foreign policy (relations with other nations).[1] Christians might add a theological or supernatural model to those; but in any case, we may not allow children to grow up ignorant of what goes on around them. From the microscopic to the indescribably vast, this is our world, and we need to find our connections with it.

Chapter 3:   Thinking Backwards
(The Way of the Reason)

Let's go back to the situation with the younger phone techs. Why is it, again, that they are less likely to make the right call on a tangled repair? Is it due only to lack of experience? If, as my husband says, it's a matter of logic, don't classes in electronics or engineering give them the deductive-reasoning abilities to solve the problem? Do they just need more technical training? Better instruments? Or is there something lacking in their overall education? What is it that children need to be taught in order to grow into competent problem solvers, critical thinkers, decision-makers? How do they develop the attentiveness to fix their minds on a problem, and the imagination to come up with a solution?

> The object of education is to put a child in
> living touch with as much as may be of the
> life of Nature and of thought... a child has
> natural relations with a vast number of
> things and thoughts: so we must train him
> upon physical exercises, nature, handicrafts,
> science and art, and upon many living
> books...Add to this one or two keys to self

knowledge, and the educated youth goes
forth with some idea of self management,
with some pursuits, and many vital
interests.[1]

Charlotte Mason talked about two things education should do: it should form habits in people, shaping the material (physical) aspect of our lives; and it should nourish with ideas, which have spiritual impact (and which affect our material side as well).

If habits are our wheels, chassis and engine, ideas are our "motive power of life," the fuel that drives us. We need to choose the right fuel and then use it to power not only the "why" but the "how" and the "what" in teaching.

Sound teaching, which habituates the mind
to move logically, must be adapted to it, and
the corresponding stages of each lesson are:
Preparation, recalling the old, and directing
the attention towards the new; Presentation
of the new matter, to all the senses as far as
possible; Association of the particulars and
that which is essential in each; and
Formulation, the expressing of the result
attained in good plain English. (S. De
Brath, *Parents' Review*) [2]

Take nature study as an example: our motivation, to quote Mason, is that a young child should have a living personal acquaintance with the things he sees, know their appearances and where to find them.[3] We want him to care; to find interest and meaning in the world around him; even to think about ecology and stewardship, if he sees pollution or damage to a natural area. So we take him to places where he can make that acquaintance in a natural context. We find out where to find things, or we find people who know and can help us. We watch the seasons; we encourage him to keep notes and press leaves, even paint them with watercolours. But we don't lecture him. We don't do boring things that will make him hate nature study forever.

In the same way, when we think about books, what is our ultimate aim? We want the child to learn to love books. Looking on the negative side, what things would you do to make someone hate books and reading forever? Make him read only little bits at a time, keep interrupting, and then lecture afterward? Water it down so that nobody could ever find the language or the story interesting? So we do the opposite: we let the child use his own mind to deal with a book, even a difficult one, and we don't take out all the interesting bits. We don't tell him that he is too young to understand.

If we say that we respect a child's dignity and individuality, his right to think for himself, we have to teach in a way that reflects that. If we believe that he has the potential for steady, regular growth, then all our teaching subjects need to follow that idea. I'm thinking of a root-bound houseplant that is transplanted into a larger pot, which then begins to grow rapidly. When we give a child that wider space, he may surprise us.

Three Tools of Learning

So how should a student learn, if learning is forming habits that are going to affect the decisions he makes and the things he does? Charlotte Mason knew of many ways to change behaviour, but most of those were methods she did not want to use. The science that was opening doors to education could equally open doors to manipulation and abuse. She refused to interfere with the child's right to be a self-determining person, with the right to act according to his own sense of moral duty. Threats were both unacceptable and ineffective; you could scare a person into behaving, but it would either make him want to escape, or break his will.

The opposite, making love or friendship a condition, was equally deplorable. So was emphasis on competition and prizes. The personal influence of a strong teacher could definitely change someone's behaviour, and probably for the better in some respects; but what would happen when that teacher was gone and the student did not know how to think for herself? None of these methods were respectful of a young human being's moral rights.

For Charlotte Mason, that left only three options:

> the Atmosphere of Environment,
> the Discipline of Habit,
> and the Presentation of Living Ideas.

Atmosphere, the Air We Breathe

> ...not an environment [meaning] a set of
> artificial relations carefully constructed, but
> an atmosphere which nobody has been at
> pains to constitute. It is there, about the
> child, his natural element, precisely as the
> atmosphere of the earth is about us...stirred
> by events, sweetened by love, ventilated,
> kept in motion, by the regulated action of
> common sense. (*Philosophy of Education*) [4]

Children learn what they live. Charlotte Mason spent the whole first section of *Home Education* talking about a healthy home environment, free from dangers and health risks, but without harmful amounts of child-centeredness. How do you deal with a toddler's bump on the knee and the resultant tears, for example? You fix the knee, but discourage the tears, not so much by telling him it doesn't hurt as by distracting his thoughts. Don't you want him to be in touch with his feelings? Yes, but you also want him to begin being able to cope with small discomforts, not to make it worse by dwelling on the pain.

In Dorothy Canfield Fisher's novel *Understood Betsy*, the main character lives, at first, with an aunt who reads all the right parenting books and takes correspondence courses in child psychology.[5] When Elizabeth Ann, later called Betsy, has a nightmare or some other fearful experience, she is encouraged to tell it all to Aunt Frances; and the narrator admits that Elizabeth Ann doesn't mind embellishing. Everything that makes Aunt Frances afraid, like big dogs, must make her afraid too. Obviously this is not a natural or a healthy environment, and yet Aunt Frances only wants to protect Elizabeth Ann.

When Elizabeth Ann suddenly has to go and stay with country cousins, she is dropped into an atmosphere which is also loving, but which nobody has been at particular "pains to constitute" for her. As she gains more confidence and self-direction, she begins to be "Betsy," a girl who cares for others and who shows real character. It's clear which atmosphere Fisher thought was healthier for children.

The Discipline of Habit

Very important, but we'll talk about it in Chapter Five.

Living Ideas: Things Alive and Growing

> We have in the child not the blank paper nor
> the plastic wax, but a growing soul which
> looks out on its surroundings with an eager
> desire to know exactly what they are. (S. De
> Brath, *Parents' Review*) [6]

Real Things are important in education. A Charlotte Mason education can and should have lots of hands-on, feet-on, five-sense activity. It should have maps and globes, marbles, dominoes, math beans, coins, paint boxes, games of tag, costumes, trips to the pond, singing, balloon rockets, socks to sort, boxes and sliding boards in the yard, clay and soap to sculpt. And even more importantly, it should present things in their own habitats: flowers, water, hills, earthworms and caterpillars.

In the nineteenth century, there was a popular educational method called the Object Lesson. This was not as simple as bringing a bird's nest for Show-and-Tell. The teacher chose the object, and the children were to describe it systematically and formally, using adjectives such as opaque, brittle, malleable (or whatever applied to a bird's nest). Some people would be quite happy to have a child express himself with such a vocabulary, but that's not the point. Charlotte Mason thought that qualities such as opacity and malleability were not what children would mention naturally; and that association with a dreary lesson ruined any interest they might still have in birds' nests.

When we talk without forcing a lesson, "about the lock in the river, the mowing machine, the ploughed field," adjectives describing colour, texture, even opacity, will enter into the conversation as well, but in their natural places. We want children not just to name the right adjectives or attributes, but to know the things themselves, the things that offer "real seed to the mind of a child."[7]

> You wonder about life on distant worlds if
> there is any life on them, the extravagances

35

of nature there...and now on this distant
world that is yours and that you have
awakened to, you will see it all for yourself.
You have only to look through this rain-
washed glass to see what astronomers from
other worlds would travel light-years to see:
this third planet from the sun... (Frederick
Buechner) [8]

Living Ideas: How Do We Use Books?

The one indispensable factor is books—the right kind of books, a
rich, varied, generous serving that causes the reader to want more.
And using those books in a way that makes use of all the habits and
skills, intelligence and imagination, powers of attention and
observation, that are already in our children and that are being built
up by the training we have been giving them.

In *Understood Betsy*, the main character is surprised, during her first
day in a country school, to be not only allowed but expected to read
more than a line at a time out loud—just as she is surprised, in
another scene, to be invited to drink all the milk she wants. The
teacher tests her further by having her read the poem "Barbara
Frietchie," and the other children stop their work to listen (and are
not scolded for listening). That evening as Betsy recounts her day to
the supposedly ignorant "Putney cousins" with whom she has come
to stay, they suggest that she read to them from Scott's *Lady of the
Lake*. Their mutual enjoyment of "The Stag at Eve" creates the first
real bond between Betsy and her new family.

What Books?

There are no short cuts, magic machines, or potions that can take the
place of good books, well served at the right time. And there is no
magic clicker to tell exactly what those are and when. Even Charlotte
Mason hesitated to give a definitive list, because she didn't want
people just taking such a list and trying to plug it in, "make it work."
In reaction to this, there was an idea going around awhile back that it
didn't matter at all what we used, that any curriculum could be used
in a Charlotte Mason style, and so we had children trying to narrate

from school readers and so on. Like putting dry rice into a slow cooker, with no liquid—it just didn't work. There is a lot of flexibility in Charlotte Mason; but it is important to choose quality books and other resources. But it's not about the booklist, in the end; it's about awakening to the possibilities of books.

> ... knowledge is acquired only by what we may call "the act of knowing," which is both encouraged and tested by narration, and which further requires the later test and record afforded by examinations. This is nothing new, you will say, and possibly no natural law in action appears extraordinarily new; we take flying already as a matter of course; but though there is nothing surprising in the action of natural laws, the results are exceedingly surprising, and to that test we willingly submit these methods.[9]

In other words: yes, reading and narration are natural; they're compatible with the way we're hardwired! Why should we be so amazed if we put the right pieces together and they actually work? That is not to say that learning is a mechanical process—fit this here, solder this here and you'll have an educated child—but only that this approach to education fits who we are and how we are made. To go back to our friend's non-functioning telephone: a technician might think of several possible approaches to the problem, and even try some temporary fixes, but in the end the only way to fix it is at the source of the actual trouble (or, as I said, by laying down new lines).

Power Tools

> This is the sort of thing that the children should go through, more or less, in every lesson—a tracing of effect from cause, or of cause from effect; a comparing of things to find out wherein they are alike, and wherein they differ; a conclusion as to causes or

consequences from certain premises. (*Home Education*) [10]

It is quite true that good laws, benevolent enterprises, great inventions, are the outcome of Reason... (*Ourselves*) [11]

When I was in eighth grade, all the girls had to take one term of Industrial Arts. (The boys spent the term making pizza and sewing football pillows.) The classroom smelled of wood shavings, and it was populated with power tools: a band saw, a belt sander, a drill press. Some of these machines were as big as I was. But it was use them or flunk, so I learned to use them. I made a flowerpot shelf, a plastic knife, and a peg game. (Years later, my husband used the peg game for an electrical board with one of the girls. Everything has its uses.)

A due recognition of the function of reason should be an enormous help to us all in days when the air is full of fallacies, and when our personal modesty, that becoming respect for other people which is proper to well-ordered natures whether young or old, makes us [too] willing to accept conclusions duly supported by public opinion or by those whose opinions we value.[12]

The Way of the Reason is also a power tool. Like a preteen girl confronting a band saw, Charlotte Mason sometimes seemed ambivalent or overly cautious about using it. Although she often paired it with the Way of the Will, she spent less time discussing it, and never seemed quite ready to trust it, as if (like a wayward power tool) it might not only take over the workshop, but escape out the door and cause havoc. But this may have been not so much because the tool was unfamiliar, but because she had seen how much damage it could do if misused. Like our shop teacher, she emphasized that this power tool needed to be respected and carefully handled. We can use Reason well to make things that are beautiful and useful; or we can ignore what the teacher says and hurt ourselves. However, Reason isn't a bad thing. We need it, and at times we may feel the world would certainly benefit by a bigger dose of Rationality and Reason; but it should not do the job of the Will.

Overanalyzing Things

Another hesitancy that Charlotte Mason had about Reason might have been that its usefulness was already quite well recognized, probably too much so. In 1869, Charles Kingsley had published his charming but complicated children's book *Madam How and Lady Why*, in which he attempts to explain Analysis vs. Synthesis.[13] Analysis, for Kingsley, meant a purely scientific way of examining things, and he represented it by someone who would "take to pieces everything he found, and find out how it was made." Analysis concentrates on parts, like a doctor who examines your sore back but doesn't relate the ache to your overall health. Synthesis gives things a more "whole-istic" consideration; it doesn't mean something artificial, but putting together rather than pulling apart.

Kingsley referred to a time when Synthesis became a "conceited tyrant" who snatched away what Analysis was doing, put it back together wrong, locked him up and starved him, and that "all honest folk welcomed him" when Analysis escaped from his prison. This would have gone over the heads of most children, but adult readers would have understood: there were certainly times in history when scientific reason was the underdog, but it had returned to the forefront. Natural Science was a hot topic of Kingsley's era, and Scientific Men were the new heroes. Kingsley said he looked forward to a time when Synthesis and Analysis would no longer cause division, but would be seen as equally important. But that hadn't happened by the time Charlotte Mason was writing her books; in fact, in parts of Europe, Synthesis was becoming increasingly strangled.[14]

Applying the Way of the Reason

> The teacher's part is, in the first place, to see
> what is to be done, to look over the work of
> the day in advance and see what mental
> discipline, as well as what vital knowledge,
> this and that lesson afford; and then to set

such questions and such tasks as shall give
full scope to his pupils' mental activity.
(*School Education*) [15]

We are responsible for making sure that the students have lots of opportunity to engage (that favourite word of educationalists) with the material—that they have to think. Some of the Parents' Union School lesson plans from a hundred years ago demonstrate this admirably. In a science lesson that compares starfish and sea-urchins (or sand dollars), we find this little etymological puzzle:

> Step V.—Let the girls compare the outer
> covering of the two creatures...Tell the girls
> that it is from this peculiar skin that this
> family is named (for by this time they will
> see that they are related), and that you want
> them to try to find out the name of the
> family for themselves. Tell them that the
> meaning of the word "sea-urchin" is derived
> from the French word *oursin*—hedgehog,
> also that the Greek word for hedgehog is
> *echinos*. Ask them the meaning of the word
> "epidermis," *epi* = upon, *derma* = skins, and
> from this perhaps they will be able to come
> to something like the name
> "Echinodermata."[16]

Would it not have been quicker to simply tell the children the name of the family? Of course. Would they have remembered it? Probably not. Would I recognize the different types of sandpaper so many years later, if I hadn't had to sand and sand and sand my peg game? Probably not.

Reason is a tool we use to examine, evaluate and organize ideas; and certainly we need it, just as the Industrial Arts room needed its band saw and drill press. Recently my eighth grader and I worked on a short section from Mortimer J. Adler's *How to Read a Book*, which pertains not only to reading but to all communication. How do you say "I understand what you said, but I disagree," without prejudice or undue emotion, but with enough specific details to support your position? And how do you deal with the fact that some people will, no matter what, resent the fact that you're disagreeing, because nice people shouldn't be disagreeable? Adler points out the difference between disagreeing with someone (because they are under-informed, misinformed, or haven't analyzed the case logically or thoroughly enough), and just being contentious.[17] (How many adults do you know who don't seem ever to have learned this?)

Minds More Awake

Chapter 4: Aladdin's Cave

> Naturally, each of us possesses this mind-
> stuff only in limited measure, but we know
> where to procure it; for the best thought the
> world possesses is stored in books; we must
> open books to children, the best books; our
> own concern is abundant provision and
> orderly serving.[1]

In Elizabeth Enright's novel *The Four-Story Mistake*, the Melendy family moves to an old house full of secret rooms and hidden treasures. One of these is a cellar room full of Victorian leftovers, including a penny-farthing bicycle, wooden sleds, and bound volumes of *Harper's Young People*. Oliver, the youngest Melendy, discovers this room by himself and keeps it a secret for a while; but he soon shows it to his sister Randy, and eventually to the rest of the family (for a Christmas present). The name of the chapter is "Ali Baba Oliver."[2]

Charlotte Mason began her last book, *Philosophy of Education*, with a sense that time was running out. She wrote as an old woman who saw the world changing rapidly, but who knew she had something valuable to offer.

> Here on the very surface is the key to that
> attention, interest, literary style, wide

vocabulary, love of books and readiness in
speaking, which we all feel should belong to
an education that is only begun at school
and continued throughout life; these are the
things that we all desire, and how to obtain
them is some part of the open secret I am
labouring to disclose "for public use." [3]

Charlotte Mason discovered an Aladdin's cave of philosophy,
method, and ideas. The only real task of an educator, according to
Mason, was to open the doorway to the cave, and to allow students
to take freely from the best ideas. She meant here the big ideas, the
ones that affect character and conduct. There are other types of
ideas, such as sensory information, but here we are looking for the
light bulbs going on, the habit makers and life changers. Not that the
teachers have to choose them painstakingly from the treasury and
hand them to the children, colour by colour or shape by shape; in
fact, that's exactly what we mustn't do. If that doesn't cause damage,
it at least wastes time, both theirs and ours. If the thing that that child
most needs today just happens to be in the next chapter of the
book—and if it's a good book, that's quite likely—then he takes what
he needs, and we don't have to schedule "Idea #42" for some other
day when he may not even be interested. This is the opposite of the
Herbartian mindset (see below), which worries that the teacher must
be somehow aware of every question that's on a child's mind, and
must have the right idea available, like a prescription, ready to drop in
when needed.

But there are other caves out there too, and not all of them
contain genuine treasure. Mason said that people exiting the others
are noticeably lacking in "initiative, the power of reflection and the
sort of moral imagination that enables you to 'put yourself in his
place.'" We could stretch the metaphor to say that the contents of at
least some of the other caves are like dull, gray colouring pages, with
a jumbo box of gray crayons for added interest.

Charlotte Mason's friend Miss Ambler said:

Our work, then, is to present to the child
such vivifying ideas as shall colour all his
thoughts, his judgments, and his actions, and

enable him to fulfill the duties and
responsibilities he inherits with his privileges
as an English citizen.[4]

As to the danger of becoming arrogant because we think we have
found the treasure, Charlotte Mason responded:

It is only in so far as Knowledge is dear to
us and delights us for herself that she yields
us lifelong joy and contentment. He who
delights in her, not for the sake of showing
off, and not for the sake of excelling others,
but just because she is so worthy to be
loved, cannot be unhappy.[5]

Our business as teachers is to make full use of what is in that
treasure cave, rather than ignoring it, or pretending it doesn't matter,
or thinking that the children won't appreciate it enough to make the
effort worthwhile. The real danger is that a generation raised on gray
crayons may forget that other colours even exist.

Don't Blame it on Herbart

I just bought a purse at the thrift store. It's in great condition, nice
and shiny, navy blue. The only problem with it is that it has too many
pockets and compartments. I don't know where to put my lip balm
or my keys, and then I can't find them again once they're in there.

People like to compartmentalize and categorize. It makes things
neat, simple, clear. We label boxes, and create computer subfolders
inside of subfolders. Some categorizing is necessary; as children learn
about universals and particulars so that they can stop calling every
four-footed animal "horsie." However, the urge to organize
everything can be overdone, especially when it comes to knowledge
(and purses).

Charlotte Mason taught and wrote two or three generations after
Johann Friedrich Herbart, a German educationalist. Although
Herbart died in 1841, his ideas became popular in Britain at the end
of the Victorian era. To those who thought the old classical ideals
were a bit elitist, Herbartianism appeared to be more democratic,
contemporary, and suitable for working-class students. It also seemed

ideal for schools where books were scarce. Herbartian methods, or at least the popular version of them, set the standard for twentieth-century teaching.

You would gather that Mason tended to disagree with his educational beliefs, or at least with the direction in which they were steering the schools, especially since she brought up his name right away, in her list of educational principles. She said,

> We hold with him entirely as to the
> importance of great formative ideas in the
> education of children, but we add to our
> ideas, habits, and we labour to form habits
> upon a physical basis. Character is the result
> not merely of the great ideas which are given
> to us, but of the habits which we labour to
> form upon those ideas.[6]

Herbart, like Charlotte Mason, believed in the importance of "great formative ideas" in the education of children. Herbart was very much about ideas: how they get into our minds, how we remember or forget them, how we prioritize and make sense of information. And not just little "scraps of information," as Charlotte Mason called them, but "great formative ideas." This is not something that we immediately associate with Herbartian teachers: their tagline is supposed to be that "it's not what children learn so much as how they learn it." So how do those seemingly contradictory ideas line up; and what can we do with them?

Charlotte Mason's tenth principle says that

> The Herbartian philosophy of education lays
> the stress of education—the preparation of
> knowledge in enticing morsels, presented in
> due order—upon the teacher.

She agreed that the knowledge offered was important, enticing, and orderly. Her complaint was that it was all about teaching and the teacher, not about learning and the child's experience. She described Herbartian teaching as one carefully measured drop at a time, at the teacher's discretion. For minds truly to awaken, something had to happen that she called the "act of knowing," and it took place inside the learner's mind.

> To "instruct" (*instruere*) is to build up—not
> knowledge—but the mind. It alone can be
> instructed. It is not a rag-bag for storing
> odds and ends, nor even a set of pigeon-
> holes where every item finds its fit place, but
> a living thing, and the characteristic of life is
> "function," action. (S. De Brath, *Parents'*
> *Review*) [7]

Now, we need to be careful about over-blaming Herbart here. Obviously Charlotte Mason had gained this opinion of the Herbartian methods, and she felt she had something more to offer, both in the way that information was presented, and in her insistence that habit should be added to ideas. Response not only in thought but in action, conduct and character, was essential. But Sir John Adams, the author of *Herbartian Psychology Applied to Education* (a book that Mason quoted from herself), insisted that Herbartianism was *not* about teachers stuffing information into brains in the same way that I pack keys and tickets and library cards into my purse. [8]

So let's leave the stuffing (or dropping) aside, and see if we can pinpoint the real divide between Charlotte Mason and Herbart.

Sir John Adams said,

> On this view, the function of the teacher
> becomes clear; for, unlike most
> Psychologies, Herbart's has an obvious and
> immediate bearing upon education. The soul
> is in the teacher's hands, inasmuch as the
> apperception masses can be made and
> modified by the teacher...During the process
> of education when the soul happens to be
> on the lookout for a certain idea, the
> teacher, knowing what is going on in the
> soul, and the laws according to which its
> mechanism work, can readily increase the

presentative activity of the idea in question
and send it right up to the dome...

Do we want to let even a well-intentioned, eminently capable teacher pry into our heads? To have our souls "made and modified" in her hands like a lump of play clay? Charlotte Mason recognized that we not only have our own thoughts, but also have a right to our own thoughts.

> ...we may not intrude upon the minds and
> overrule the wills of others...it is indecent to
> let another probe the thoughts of the
> "unconscious mind" whether of child or
> man.[9]

And here is the second difference, a very important one: how are ideas and memories organized in our minds? Are they compartmentalized (though hard to access), like the keys and pens in my new purse, or all jumbled together, randomly surfacing? Mrs. Dowson put it very well in a *Parents' Review* article:

> When knowledge has been organized...the
> multitudinous parts of knowledge are
> already wrought together into a living fabric
> instead of being tied up in isolated packets
> with mental red-tape, and pigeon-holed in
> out-of-the-way departments of the
> Circumlocution Office of a mechanical
> brain.[10]

Herbartianism sees knowledge organized in neatly divided areas of thought, often referred to as faculties or apperception masses. If you have an existing apperception mass for Canadian history, then any new fact you learn about the 1837 Rebellion will attach itself to the right spot, in a sort of brain blob tag. Charlotte Mason agreed that incoming ideas needed to find "pegs" to hang themselves on; she agreed with Herbart that learning must always begin with what is already known. But she wanted to do away not only with the idea of multiple compartments, but with the entire purse metaphor. Her ninth principle says:

We hold that the child's mind is no
mere *sac* to hold ideas; but is rather, if the
figure may be allowed, a spiritual organism,
with an appetite for all knowledge. This is its
proper diet, with which it is prepared to
deal; and which it can digest and assimilate
as the body does foodstuffs.

A Hundred Lovely Landscapes

This is how any child's mind works, and our
concern is not to starve these fertile
intelligences. They must have food in great
abundance and variety...pictures by great
artists old and new...Perhaps we might
secure at least a hundred lovely landscapes
too,—sunsets, cloudscapes, starlight
nights. *(Philosophy of Education)* [11]

I said earlier that there were reasons other than health for getting
children outside whenever possible. In *Home Education*, Charlotte
Mason said that the business of a young child is "to find out all he
can with his senses." The particular form of outdoor time she
recommended focused on both nature study and hands-on physical
geography, exploring what is out there, noticing landscapes and
farmyards, shadows and wind. These afternoons outside sound
something like Scout meetings, with time at the beginning for
blowing off steam, and at the end for games, but with the bulk of the
afternoon for children "finding out all they can."

What did they study? Everything that grew in their outing-area:
wild flowers, crops, trees, birds, tadpoles, and caterpillars (taken
home in a jar). They were to experiment with distance and direction
(how long does it take to run from one hedge to another?), and
understand a bit about maps. The adult(s) could use local landforms
to teach them geography. In *Home Education*, Mason assumed that
there was one mother getting outdoors with several children of
different ages, which would not necessarily describe every family
situation even at that time. The whole thing might seem less

daunting, more do-able, if two or three families got together regularly and did these learning times as a group.

Meet Mrs. Dowson

Mary Emily Dowson was the first female surgeon registered in England. She wrote several articles for the *Parents' Review*, modestly signing herself "Mrs. Dowson." As a doctor and scientist, you would think that Mrs. Dowson would be firmly on the side of logical, give-me-the-facts math and science education. However, science education, as she saw it taught, depended too much on "the brute scientific fact."

> Botany, for example, is usually taught in
> schools just as the lists of kings and queens
> were taught to our grandmothers: it is taught
> as a more or less cooked-up arrangement of
> brute facts about plants, their characters,
> their structure and their functions, served
> with a sauce of scientific moralizing about
> heredity and environment and the like.[12]

Mrs. Dowson respected science too much to want to see it taught in such a cookbook fashion, with many facts but little understanding. She cared about analysis, but didn't want to see it taught alone, without synthesis. She said that nature, or our experience of reality, "defies our exactness and makes a mock of our descriptions." Like Job listening to God's "were you there" questions, we need to respond with humility. There are things in the universe that we don't understand, and even the best scientists may know a great deal of Madam How but still not come close to Lady Why.

We might compare that to the way Shakespeare's plays are sometimes taught in the classroom: footnoted to pieces with lines, scenes, metre, and pathetic fallacy, but without a sense of the whole story. Knowing the facts of science, having read many books or watched hours of documentaries, does not give one the qualities of a scientist, but in fact may make us as arrogant as Cousin Eustace in *Voyage of the Dawn Treader*.[13] What was Mrs. Dowson's proposed solution? More required physics courses?

If we were tied down to a choice between
science and letters...we should choose
letters....those great organizers of our chaotic
democracy of knowledge—the subjects
which treat of the mind of man, of his
knowing, feeling and acting, and of cause
and purpose and meaning in the great whole
of things.

What is it she said that was going to organize our knowledge?
"Letters." What are "letters?" As she defined them, the subjects
dealing with how people know, feel, and act; the meaning, the
purpose, the wholeness. We do not need to offer a special
elementary-level course in learning to think, but (*please read this and get
very excited here!*) Mrs. Dowson said that we do need to teach

the art of bringing all they learn, science,
letters and what not, into some approach to
a unified, inter-related whole. If we can
effect this, we shall be able to put into the
hands of a child an instrument of moral as
well as of mental discipline, and a piece of
work to do that nobody else, great or small,
has done or ever can do for him.

Charlotte Mason agreed:

No one knoweth the things of a man but the
spirit of a man which is in him; therefore,
there is no education but self-education, and
as soon as a young child begins his
education he does so as a student.[14]

Don't Expect Them To Do It All Themselves

Whether you know the names of these parts
now does not matter. I want you to *see* them.
(St. Augustine, *Of the Teacher*) [15]

We, the teachers, are not bringing everything children learn into wholeness *for* them. We are teaching them the art of bringing what they learn into relationship for themselves, of seeing the wholeness and making the connections. We are putting the tools into their hands. However, sometimes the teacher actually has to teach the art of putting those connections in order.

For instance, in a geography lesson about types of soil, the teacher should end by showing (not naming) each sample and having the class state its characteristics; then name each sample, describe its qualities, and have the class repeat the name.[16] (St. Augustine would surely approve.)

In a history lesson about Roman Britain, what is it that we really want students to see in their minds, to be able to call up afterward? We would like them to be able to place the major Roman roads and garrisons on a mental map of England, and demonstrate their grasp of this by adding them to a blank map. So the essential points, the things they need to understand in order to put the forts and roads in the right spots, are "the mountains and plains with their properties, the fords of the rivers, the roads...the communication with Gaul, and so with Rome."[17] "Forts" may sound a bit dreary, but the point is that they don't pop up randomly. If a city was founded on the site of a fort or a castle, there had to have been a reason it was just there. Maybe it was at the top of a hill, or it protected a point such as the mouth of a river. To give a Canadian example, after you have studied the travels of the French explorers along the St. Lawrence River, the locations of Quebec City and Montreal make sense; and if you know that Halifax is where ships come in and go out across the Atlantic, you will not likely place it on the wrong side of Nova Scotia.

> Every new bit of knowledge we acquire
> should make a difference to every other bit
> we possess, and should itself, in its turn, be
> modified by all the rest. (Mrs. Dowson) [18]

What Kind of Books are Best?

> [We must] trust, not to our own teaching,
> but to the best that we have in art and
> literature... (*Philosophy of Education*) [19]

How do we determine the contents of the treasure trove? Is there a list of the best one hundred books, even a crucial few? Does *Watership Down* rank above *Westward Ho!*? What if we have special interests or non-interests, religious, geographical, or otherwise? What if a person we respect doesn't approve of fairy tales? How subjective should the choosing be?

Charlotte Mason never wanted to give too-pat answers about anything. By her ambivalence about listing particular books, she unintentionally fostered a long-standing gulf between those who say "Charlotte Mason refused to list particular books for children, so there is no such thing as a Charlotte Mason curriculum," and those who point to the fact that she did indeed spearhead a complete curriculum, with a long list of books.[20] Even in those days, though, one imagines the reaction—"Make it easier for us! Give us some examples!" She insisted that

> we cannot make any hard and fast rule—a
> big book or a little book, a book at first-
> hand or at second-hand; either may be right
> provided we have it in us to discern a living
> book, quick [*meaning full of life, not speedy*], and
> informed with the ideas proper to the
> subject of which it treats.[21]

That doesn't mean that she didn't make suggestions, and even assumptions, that certain books, poems, paintings, and pieces of music would be included without question. Nevertheless, she left the list open to the (assumed) educated and intelligent adult who should be able to make those choices and then allow the books to give the increase. What seems to matter most is whether a book has the power to awaken ideas, stir up curiosity, help children to look outside themselves and see the world in new ways.

Not Everything is Fiction

Emphasizing literary form in lessons does not mean that we don't teach grammar and chemistry. It does mean that Mrs. Dowson, for example, saw more importance for the arts and humanities in a child's education, than she did for "brute facts." If the ideas are there, the facts come along naturally; but denuded facts just curl up and die.

We have a hard time learning them without context, or at least remembering them for longer than the term test.

One of the books we used in our homeschool was *How Did We Find Out About Electricity?* by Isaac Asimov.[22] As a child, I doubt that I ever wandered into the science section of the public library, and I certainly wouldn't have picked out a book about electricity. But if someone had read Asimov's book to me, I would have loved it.

> But the crackles were so small and the
> flashes of light so tiny that Guericke grew
> impatient. If he was going to carry this
> experiment further, he needed to pack more
> electricity into the amber...Carefully,
> Guericke broke the flask and removed the
> pieces of glass. He had a yellow ball of sulfur
> larger than his head, with a handle. He
> placed this ball in a wooden holder. He
> could turn the ball of sulfur by using the
> handle. If he placed his other hand on the
> sulfur as it turned, the rubbing, or friction,
> filled the sulfur with electricity. Nobody had
> ever before collected so much electricity in
> one place.

The story about Otto von Guericke is full of sparks, crackles, and flashes of light. It's about the idea that energy is something you can collect up, and that it might be able to produce even more energy if you just had an even bigger ball and could turn it around even faster. It's about where ideas come from, and the fact that other scientists built onto Guericke's discovery.

> Because knowledge is power, the child who
> has got knowledge will certainly show power
> in dealing with it. He will recast, condense,
> illustrate, or narrate with vividness and with
> freedom the arrangement of his words. The
> child who has got only information will

write and speak in the stereotyped phrases
of his text-book, or will mangle in his notes
the words of his teacher. (*School Education*) [23]

Not Everything is Old

It's safe to say that, going by some of Charlotte Mason's frequent references, she would have counted a child's education as incomplete that didn't include the Bible, Plutarch's *Lives*, Scott's novels, and Wordsworth's poems. In *Home Education*, she mentioned *Treasure Island*, *Robinson Crusoe*, and stories from the Odyssey as being appropriated by young children for their play; and she listed *Pilgrim's Progress*, *Tanglewood Tales*, and *Heroes of Asgard*.[24] For the younger set she also recommended books of travel and exploration, and Holden's *The Sciences*, which "makes so fit an approach to the sensible and intelligent mind of a child."[25] These are just the most basic of Mason's must-haves, from the nursery-and-governesses period.

However, not everything that is old is good; and not everything that is good, is old. My husband fixes old radios and clocks. Usually he works on clocks made by just one early-twentieth-century Canadian firm. Today he brought home a commercially made clock from the 1970's, which was made, surprisingly for the time, with old-fashioned brass parts, two springs and a hammer. He has the pieces out on the workbench, and he says he is surprised and impressed at how well made this clock was. He guesses it would have been sold somewhere like a jewellery store, where customers were still looking for wind-up works instead of automatic quartz.

In the same way, making a list of the best older books doesn't rule out new books; or out-of-print treasures nobody else seems to have heard of, or that belong to your own part of the world. One of our favourite local stories is a historical novel, *The Trail of the Conestoga*, that my grandmother read to me when I was young.[26] It tells the story of Pennsylvania-German settlers in our area, some of them related to us. We've also searched out books about Ontario wildflowers, local birds, and other interesting things found along the Grand River. It's enlightening to see your small corner of the world in print.

Applying This Chapter with Younger Students

Chapter XVII of *Parents and Children* is a fun one. Although Charlotte Mason talked so much elsewhere about ideas that come from books, she said here,

> We all recognise that the training of the
> senses is an important part of education.

However, this is not about teaching children to settle for "nice" or "yucky." It's getting a sense of what makes sense in the world. When you are watching out the window on the coldest winter day, you might notice the biggest, noisiest crows you've ever seen, flying up into the tallest trees in the neighbourhood. When spring finally comes, you notice softer air, sweeter scents, and longer days. Using comparative terms is a natural part of conversation! But you can take shades and degrees of things even further: at the paint store, you can look at a hundred tints and shades of blue. You can think about why the snow melts more quickly on the driveway than on the lawn; you can sniff the milk to see if it's gone off, or the cookies to know that they're done. And when you're done looking and smelling, you can start in on sounds. This is a process of observation, examination, estimation, and classification; this is about being scientists and detectives, nature scouts, even mathematicians.

For instance, what everyday things do your children already associate with a standard unit of measurement? We often have children measure their feet or arms, or weigh themselves, and that is interesting, but it can also be confusing because children are growing, and one child's feet are bigger than another's. What less-variable sizes or weights of things can they become aware of, to give them a comparison? Some girls own eighteen-inch dolls; others have eleven-and-a-half-inch fashion dolls, and that is close to a foot. If you know that the doll is twelve or eighteen inches tall, you will not then guess that a pencil is twenty-four inches long.

Another common measurement is standard paper (again about a foot long). Maybe it would help to know how tall your dog is, with four feet on the ground; is that taller than the table? How high are the ceilings? How tall is Dad? Is that round thing the size of a golf ball, a baseball, or a basketball? In our family we used Cuisenaire rods for math, which range in length from one to ten centimeters; a side benefit of using these is that we now just say "about as long as an orange rod."[27] A mental measuring tape can help when you need to describe something new.

Cooks used to use more comparative terms: butter the size of an egg, balls of dough the size of a walnut. Does that make cooking easier or harder? Would you want to drink a whole quart (or liter) of lemonade? What would a pound (or a kilogram) of chocolate or nuts look like? A pound or a kilogram of potatoes?

There is a cooking lesson at the very end of Charlotte Mason's *School Education*, where teenage girls are taught to make "little cakes," and one of the objectives is "To give them opportunity of thinking for themselves why certain things should be done." If they want the cakes sweeter, richer, bigger, smaller, what will they have to change? What are the non-negotiables if they want "little cakes" and not something else?

This sort of practical lesson combines with the measurement and estimation activities mentioned earlier. What does a cupful of flour look like, and how many servings will, say, a pancake recipe calling for one cupful of flour make? What sorts of flour do we have, and which one(s) do we want to use for these pancakes? Do we want to make the batter very sweet? Probably not. Last time we made pancakes we used soured milk and baking soda to make them rise; should we try fresh milk and baking powder this time, and see if they turn out much differently? Do they cook better if the pan is very hot at the beginning, or just medium-hot? What is the best way to keep them from sticking to the pan? What will we serve on top?

Muffins are also a great choice for infinite variation: they can be sweet or hardly sweet at all, whole wheat or wheat-free, and can incorporate many fruits or even vegetables, cheese, and meat. My oldest daughter emailed me recently to ask for my basic oatmeal muffin recipe, complaining that I had posted so many "I sort of made this one up" variations on our family blog that she couldn't find the original.

This exercise in decision-making is in contrast to children's cooking activities that involve smearing canned icing on pre-baked cupcakes, and adding candies on top. Working with real food is a more worthwhile use of children's time than, if you will excuse the expression, a "canned" activity.

Applying This Chapter with Older Students

Once we've practiced communicating sensory details such as "about as hot as tap water" and "I think a skunk was around here last night," we have another type of idea to work on: feelings.

> Let us consider carefully what feelings we
> wish to stimulate or repress in our children,
> and then, having made up our minds, let us
> say nothing.[28]

Nothing? What did Charlotte Mason mean, say nothing? First, the feelings she described are not simple emotions of happiness or sadness; they are not moral or immoral; they are not feelings of love or justice that need an object; they are more like perceptions. Here's the list (with opposites): pleasure, displeasure; appreciation, depreciation; anticipation, foreboding; admiration, contempt; assurance, hesitancy; diffidence, complacency; and other things that are equally hard to put into words.

If we say nothing, how do we educate the feelings? Well, there is example. We can show appreciation, reverence, and admiration. How do we handle a special book or piece of china, or remove an adhesive bandage as gently as possible? How do we get ready for a special day? It is not even always in the act, but in the feeling that is communicated without words. I remember visiting a large art gallery with a school group, many years ago. One of the girls had a particular interest in art, and I overheard her, as we left, saying to her mother, "Oh, Mom!" And her mother answered, "I know." That's all they had to say; there was a strong sympathy of feeling between them.

Though it's hard to find definite ways to educate these feelings, it's not nearly as hard to crush them. Recognizing that feelings matter, and avoiding teasing and other unfriendly situations, may represent the limit of what we can do about them.

Chapter 5:   The Gift of Discipline

...The child will bring the gift of obedience,
the parent may have to offer the service of
rebuke... (*Ourselves*) [1]

In Louisa May Alcott's novel *Eight Cousins*[2], teenaged Rose is being cared for by a clutch of aunts, all of whom have particular agendas for her. One in particular, gloomy Aunt Myra, insists on seeing Rose as sickly, and uses any excuse to dose her with favourite medicines. In a rather troubling aside, it's hinted that Aunt Myra may have "dosed" her own daughter to death. Clearly, this well-meaning woman should be given a wide berth.

But into the story comes Uncle Alec, a doctor, who takes away Rose's morning coffee and her silly dresses, and makes her go out and play and build up her constitution. He is also a believer in cold baths. Aunt Myra's medicines are to be avoided at all costs; but even Uncle Alec's would be reserved for actual sickness. Later Rose does come down with pleurisy, after standing outside too long in freezing weather, and Aunt Myra gets her chance to gloat—but not to medicate.

What Does Health Have to Do With It?

The emphatic health and dietary advice in Charlotte Mason's first volume confuses a lot of us. Advice on airing the nursery is not exactly what we're looking for in a book on education.

But however we interpret a healthy lifestyle, children can't learn well without one. And some of Mason's criticisms here are not that outdated. She mentioned children whose only lunch was aniseed drops, junk food from the corner store. She talked about the need for regular exercise. She was adamant about the idea that young children didn't spend enough time outdoors; there are books being written today about this increasing problem, and experimental "outdoor kindergartens" are popping up to combat excessive indoor-ness.[3] And the latest issue of *Scientific American* contains an article about "air pollutants in the sleep microenvironment."[4] If the physical environment is an issue, it is going to be harder to improve the other areas of life. We have more control over this if we are homeschooling our own children; but in some school situations, there will be children who didn't get a warm bubble bath last night or a hug before bed; who arrive without breakfast or without coats and mittens. There will be those who go home to stressed, unhappy parents. No matter how good the curriculum, it is harder for children to learn if their material world isn't all it should be. On the other hand, maybe those children need this education the most.

Going Out to Play

I was not an outdoorsy child. I would rather have played dolls or read books on a snowy day than be zipped into a snowsuit and banished outside. However, my mother (maybe for her own sanity) liked children to go out and play, and when I think about it, we spent a lot of time outside, back in that age when children really did play in the street until it got dark. Houses weren't air-conditioned, so in the summer it was often just as comfortable (or as uncomfortable) to be outdoors. We rode bicycles, swam at the lake, went skating after school, and walked distances alone that would have had today's child protective services at the door. When we went to Guide camp, it was in tents. With outhouses. And we survived.

For Charlotte Mason, there were multiple reasons to give children plenty of outdoor time; there were places to see, air to breathe, birds to list. Besides, unless you were sick or maybe a rich child in a city, being outdoors a lot was the normal thing (and even then, you probably got to the seaside occasionally). For now, we'll stick to the health factors: besides fresh air, there was the idea of movement, of being able to dig in the dirt, splash in the water, climb the trees. Children can jump rope and ride a tricycle in the basement, even go to a fancy indoor play park full of plastic climbers, but that's not the same as sliding down a real hill or climbing on real rocks.

Now Back to Discipline

Are you a disciplinarian? Are you disciplined?

Do you want to be?

After a harsh winter, we had to have some work done in our yard. The owner of the company told my husband that the only way he can keep the business going these days is to go out on every job and supervise everything his employees do. He said, "If I'm not there, the cell phones and the cigarettes come out." He had to tell his helper to go get the leaf blower and clean up the mess when they had finished cutting branches. *"Mumble mumble grumble." "Just go do it."* Then the employee ran the truck over our garbage that was waiting for pickup. (They did give us a discount because of the garbage.)

The word disciple has interesting connotations: discipline, disciple, following another person's teaching. It also means a code of behaviour, order, rigour, regulation, training, and eventually, growth in moral character. If we are disciplined, we are more willing to obey or more able to control ourselves, even in difficult situations; more mature, if you like.

What part does Discipline play in Uncle Alec's approach to health? We think that Uncle Alec (or Alcott) would say, like Charlotte Mason, something about Method vs. System.

> Method has a few comprehensive laws
> according to which details shape themselves,
> as one naturally shapes one's behaviour to
> the acknowledged law that fire burns.
> System, on the contrary, has an infinity of
> rules and instructions as to what you are to
> do and how you are to do it. Method in
> education follows Nature humbly; stands
> aside and gives her fair play.[5]

So yes, in those terms, parents and teachers using Charlotte Mason's methods need to be the biggest disciplinarians that ever were! What we can give is the idea to begin, and the support to continue, along with the practical tools children need. But we can't do the habits of attentiveness or the work of nature notebooking for them, any more than we can take over other people's spiritual disciplines. If there is no education but self-education, there is also no true discipline but self-discipline.

Charlotte Mason said that if she were asked about discipline-that-actually-means-punishment, she would say that punishment has a necessary time and place, like medicine. The trouble with punishment, Mason said, is that sometimes children rather enjoy it. They may even feel somewhat heroic about it if they take it stoically. And the threat of punishment, as many have noted, does not necessarily deter crime, and does not always rehabilitate the criminal. One wonders if Laura Ingalls Wilder's grandfather and his brothers ever repeated their Sunday sledding transgression, if the fun they had lessened the pain of the licking afterward. It wouldn't be such a good story without the dreaded punishment at the end.[6]

But punishment is not the same as discipline. Understanding the real consequences of a breach of law has a different effect from deciding whether you will break the rules even if it means being spanked or grounded, or even imprisoned afterward. Parental moaning that we've honestly tried, that we've nagged, coaxed and lectured but with little response, earns us a B grade. We are not absolute failures, but if we put some scientifically based muscle into the habit problem, said Charlotte Mason, we would see incredible results. Is it worth the extra struggle for an A?

On page 175 of *Parents and Children*, Mason outlined her "Habits Anonymous" program for change, including this:

> Do not tell him to do the new thing, but
> quietly and cheerfully see that he does it on
> all possible occasions, for weeks if need be,
> all the time stimulating the new idea, until it
> takes great hold of the child's imagination.

In other words, he doesn't get the option to do otherwise, at least at first. You are somehow to set circumstances up, as creatively as possible, so that the train starts going down a brand new track. Discipline is making the new way, more than thinking about the old one. It means to let the grass grow over those unused rails; and to create opportunities for the person to do the new, desired action, keeping the mind busy with a bigger and more absorbing idea than the old one. It provides a new place to go, a new activity, a way to take the misused trait or selfish desire, and redirect it. However, it is suggested that, partway through the "retraining" process, you make time to talk about it with the person involved. It's not animal training, with the parent making it all happen, or getting all the credit.

In Phyllis McGinley's story *The Plain Princess*, Princess Esmeralda goes through a transformation in attitude, and so she wants to give a great reward to Dame Goodwit, the woman who did for her what the royal parents did not (shame on them). Dame Goodwit shakes her head and says that Esmeralda really did it all herself. We could argue with that and credit the change in atmosphere when Esmeralda left the palace to live with Dame Goodwit's family. We could point out that Esmeralda was forced immediately to abandon her worst habits, only because the opportunity wasn't there (no servants to order around), and to begin doing more for herself. However, we will allow Dame Goodwit's point that Esmeralda herself found the strength to change.[7]

Faith and Habit

A note here to those who believe that since God is good and we are sinful but saved by grace, we should not attempt to encroach on the miraculous work of the Holy Spirit: this does not mean we don't ask for God's help to change, only that we see the value of personal effort as well. We can use the simple but limited example of losing weight and becoming healthier by a change in diet. If we are given the knowledge to be able to do this, and we are aware that our overeating (if that is the problem) is displeasing to God, then we are doing right to change that physical habit. We continue to give glory to God for teaching us what to do and giving us the strength to make that change. Few people would argue with that. Well, if we have the God-given knowledge to plant seeds (as it says in Scripture), and the ability to stop overeating, then we are equally free to examine intellectual, moral, and even spiritual habits. We can use the same process to liberate ourselves from laziness, or to begin a definite habit of Bible reading.

If our understanding of human nature allows us to resolve conflict well, or to teach a class well, or to change our own habits, then we should use those tools, but without saying that any of those actions are usurping God's work. It is simply making use of the natural laws of how we are made.

And if that increasing understanding also allows us to treat our children well, within the bounds of respect for individuality, then we should have no hesitation in doing so. Charlotte Mason referred to Christ's condemnation of anyone who mistreats or devalues children, and that includes every area of life: physical, intellectual, moral, spiritual.

> *These things*
> *I do despise:*
> *Hypocrisy*
> *and lies,*
> *And anything at all that dims*
> *The light in children's eyes.*
>
> (Ruth T. Stamper) [8]

Applying Discipline with Younger Students

Happy is the household that has few rules.
(*Parents and Children*) [9]

It takes discipline to start a task, and discipline to stop at the right time or the right amount. However, my bread machine does exactly those things when I push a button, and human beings aren't machines, so it's not simply a matter of having the right parameters programmed into us.

Or is it? If our habits shape us, we have accepted a certain amount of "programming," and that is not always a bad thing. Maybe children are used to taking one or two cookies, no more, and the habit puts an automatic cap on their cookie appetites. Charlotte Mason said at one point that if a girl is used to being truthful, the idea of lying to get out of trouble will not occur to her.

Mason also suggested helping children form early habits of time, place, and surroundings.[10] While it's not good for children to be too rigid (refusing to nap anywhere but their own beds), it's still important to develop basic routines and habits in the home. Wiping up and being kind are not *rules* you are forced to submit to; they're just the things you do.

Home makeovers sometimes feature babies' rooms decorated with "adult" furniture that they can grow into. Some people would consider that a waste of money; and it is probably true that Chippendale chairs are not the best choice for active little children.

However, the opposite is also true: furnishing a child's room with junk does not teach him to respect his possessions or anyone else's. It's good to teach the habit of using things carefully, or, rather, not to have to un-teach anything else; that includes the furniture, whatever household electronics and media devices children are allowed to use (such as telephones), perhaps even the car or van. Why is it now the norm that family vehicles are littered with food wrappers, any more than family living rooms?

Charlotte Mason proposed role-playing good manners with children. Later, if not sooner, they will have to sit through a wedding, a movie at a theatre, or a visit to an elderly relative. Will they be welcome guests, or nuisances?

Applying Discipline with Older Students

> [A child] should know that the duty of self-
> direction belongs to him; and that powers
> for this direction are lodged in him, as are
> intellect and imagination, hunger and thirst.
> (*Philosophy of Education*) [11]

The next group of habits in *Home Education* (Part IV) are ones that Charlotte Mason said should be taught instead of just caught. We can begin working on some of them, such as attention and obedience, at an early age. Others seem to apply more to school-aged children, such as the "mental habits," which we might not think of as habits at all.

Imagination is a habit that comes more naturally to some children than to others. When our oldest was little, she attended a neighbourhood preschool class two mornings a week. One day the teacher mentioned with concern that she had been rubbing her ear, and wondered if she might have an earache. I asked if she had been putting her hand up to her mouth as well, and the teacher said yes. "It's all right," I told her, "she's just talking on her telephone." Charlotte Mason actually mentioned that there could be a gap in imagination between children of different classes; that certain groups may benefit from kindergarten songs and stories (or perhaps educational television?), but that for children who already have lots of inner and outer imaginative stimuli, it's overkill. You may wonder why our daughter went to preschool at all, and the answer is just that she enjoyed it, the teacher was sympathetic (they had a common interest in invisible rabbits), and it gave her the chance to play with other children.

However, fantasy-imagination is not all there is; we also need to train the moral imagination, the ability to see beyond ourselves, and use that power for change. In one episode of the British television series *Foyle's War*, a character named Willis was being interviewed for a position with the secret service. The department head turned Willis down because he didn't go to the right schools. Detective Foyle remarked, "I understand we're looking for people who are astute, with an ability to see the other person's point of view." (Later in the episode, Willis proved Foyle right.)[12] The moral imagination does not mean that you are naïve, that you think only good things. If you want to be a spy or a detective, you have to learn to think like the enemy, or like a criminal. If you want to repair telephones, you have to have the imagination to think through what might be causing a problem, and to come up with possible solutions. And you cannot develop that imagination without wide experience, both the real-life, hands-on, sensory kind, and the ideas that you absorb from others, often through the medium of books.

Another "mental habit" is *Thinking*, or exercising the Way of the Reason. Then *Remembering*, a habit that is only going to become natural through lots of practice. Also *Application*, which means putting some elbow grease into the job. This leads to *Perfect Execution*, and finishing what one starts. Some of these will come into play through everyday life, chores and projects, music lessons and construction sets; but school lessons should be the most obvious place to practice good habits of mind.

Lost Treasures of Charlotte Mason, #2

Parents and Children, *Chapter VIII, "The Culture of Character: Parents as Trainers."*

Plutarch often started his *Lives* by telling anything that was known about the parents and grandparents of his subject. In the ancient world of tyrannies and democracies, coming from a noble family was very important. Charlotte Mason's world was still full of class distinctions and questions about the value of heredity. Is it true that you are saddled for life with whatever your parents pass down to you?

We'll get back to that in a minute. First, think about the things that every single person naturally wants, aside from physical needs. In Charlotte Mason's vocabulary, those things were knowledge, perfection, beauty, power, and society (human relationships). Of course children want to know things, and want to be loved. Put the opportunity for those things in front of them, and they will take them, no mystery there. You would almost think, said Mason, that the teachers could just go home, that parents could sit back and let the children do what comes naturally. And they probably wouldn't turn out so badly.

But something is missing, something that isn't handed to us in a package, and something that is an achievement, "the one practical achievement possible to us for ourselves and for our children." Mason said that if we put at least some belief in heredity, there are two things that keep our inherited faults and virtues from destroying "the balance of qualities we call sanity": the fact that we marry other people and mix up the gene pool, which doesn't concern us here; and the possibilities of "education," if education's true work is to develop character.

Now here is the crux of the chapter. Let's say that you have those natural desires which will develop themselves as opportunity comes along. And that you have certain hereditary dispositions and traits, good or bad. Charlotte Mason asked, hoping that you see she was being somewhat facetious: what is left for education to do? What's the use of trying to teach character, if so much of it is all settled? We might even feel that God made this child a certain way, and it's not up to us to interfere with God's doing, unless it seems like he's going to turn into a criminal (and then it's full throttle punishment).

> But alas, how many of us degrade the thing
> we love! Think of the multitude of innocents
> to be launched on the world, already
> mutilated, spiritually and morally, at the
> hands of doting parents.

These justifications for letting alone are all nonsense, said Charlotte Mason. If you have a rip in your pants and you own a needle and thread, why wouldn't you go ahead and fix them? Why would we feel an almost proprietary pride when Junior displays the family stubbornness, tendency to overeat, or aptitude for making a sharp deal? Whether those traits come from nature or nurture, it's time to break the cycle.

The last bit of this chapter is about gifted children, those who obviously have some special calling in one direction. This could be an intellectual talent, or it might be an unusual moral quality; instead of Grandfather's temper in the toddler, we see his love of music. Charlotte Mason had her own Gifted and Talented program: Exercise, Nourishment, Change, and Rest. She said not to discourage a gifted child from doing what comes naturally; if he wants to play the violin or learn Latin at three, he'll let you know.

> Let him do just so much as he takes to of his
> own accord; but never urge, never applaud,
> never show him off.

Chapter 6: A Philosophy of Words

> Has there ever been a time when no stories
> were told? Has there ever been a people
> who did not care to listen? I think not.
> When we were little, before we could read
> for ourselves, did we not gather eagerly
> round father or mother, friend or nurse, at
> the promise of a story? (H.E.
> Marshall, *Literature for Boys and Girls*) [1]

Charlotte Mason described delight as a chief object of education—delight in knowledge, and delight in life.

> ...Socrates conceived that knowledge is for
> pleasure, in the sense, not that knowledge is
> one source, but is *the* source of pleasure.[2]

In other words, education is for us. For our own selves, for the children, and any interested others. It is, in a way, citizenship. It shows us what it means to be people, and it teaches us how to live in the world. Charlotte Mason listed virtues that could be mined in her Aladdin's Cave: candour, fortitude, temperance, patience, meekness, courage, generosity. But we don't stand in the doorway of the cave, handing those things out one moral at a time. The feast is inside: many living books. Many ideas. Many glimpses of the divine, of

Eternity, of something beyond ourselves. But with this whole world of things and ideas to look at and think about and draw, why is it that much teaching in schools seems like tiny one-bite candy bars?

This is why Charlotte Mason emphasized many books, important books, and "living" books. In Scott's *Ivanhoe*, a hermit called the Clerk of Copmanhurst has an unwelcome visitor, the Black Knight, who needs a place to stay for the night. Because the Clerk is supposed to be living under a vow of poverty (and certainly not poaching deer in the forest), he offers the Knight a miserly little dish of dried peas for supper, and claims that this food alone miraculously sustains him. But The Black Knight is quick to see through it. He guesses that the Clerk must have more food—probably illegally come by—in the cupboard, and he gradually convinces him to share what he has hidden. (Then they become friends and have a good time.)[3] Do we so equally mistrust young students that we attempt to deceive them with a bit of "pease?"

> Something was crawling. Worse still,
> something was coming out. Edmund or
> Lucy or you would have recognized it at
> once, but Eustace had read none of the right
> books. (C.S. Lewis, *Voyage of the Dawn
> Treader*) [4]

So we read books just because they make us happy or because they're fun, because they will make us sound smart, because they'll get us into college or a good job ahead of the others? Or should we use them as a practical guide to recognizing dragons? No, they show us that we have a purpose; that we can be useful in the world, and that is our pleasure. Education gives us minds more awake, and a life that is more than just passing time.

> Leave us alone without books and we shall
> be lost....We shall not know what to join on
> to, what to cling to, what to love and what
> to hate, what to respect and what to despise.
> (F. Dostoevsky, *Notes from Underground*) [5]

On Teaching Reading (and Other Things)

If we're not looking for early reading lessons, we may skip right over those pages in *Home Education*. Even those of us who read that section years ago may not bother much with it if our children are older. And that is too bad, because there's something very important going on there.

Charlotte Mason explained the use of sight words in teaching reading by pointing out that we remember what interests us most.

> But the thing he learns to know by looking
> at it, is a thing which interests him. Here we
> have the key to reading...The child should be
> taught from the first to regard the printed
> word as he already regards the spoken word,
> as the symbol of fact or idea full of interest.[6]

Learning to read, for Charlotte Mason, was not much different from the way that a child looks at fallen leaves, and rabbits, and horribly big beetles on the sidewalk. She extended the idea (on page 243) with her opinion on why young children should not do written composition: because their business in early life is to collect material, to squirrel away ideas, not to have to write essays on them. A young student going through these early reading lessons, learning words from nursery rhymes and playing word-building games, is adding to his collection, organizing and classifying his knowledge as he would press and label flowers. A child who memorizes a poem, not line by line but by listening to the whole is, in the Augustinian sense, "seeing" it. Perhaps the educator who coined the phrase "whole language" had the right idea after all.

In a sample reading lesson, beginning readers are shown an illustration and a short passage from *The Happy Reader*, by E.L. Young.[7] This is the text they are working on:

A CABIN BOY

Ben is a cabin boy. He lives on a big ship
with turrets and guns on the deck. Ben has a
hammock in the ship, instead of a bed.

According to the plan, the teacher is to draw attention to the picture, briefly, but not read the story out loud. She writes five new words from the story on the blackboard. Then it's time for the children to do some work: they are to read those words out loud, sounding them out, then "write them in the air with their eyes shut." They then have to find those new words on the page. Using "loose letters" (manipulatives or cutouts), they are to make those words as the teacher dictates them. And then...only then...do they read those three lines from the book. If they have trouble with any of the new words, the teacher is to print them on the board again, have them form them again with their letters, and find them in the book again. This is to take about ten minutes.

So what have the children done in this lesson? Literally, they have collected some new words. They have spelled them and read them until those new words are fixed in their minds. It's very much like the landscape descriptions, or narration after a story. They look or listen carefully, and then they re-create. When they've done that, the material is theirs forever.

And who doesn't like to imagine being a cabin boy with a hammock?

Another lesson plan (from a different teacher) has a child read through the first verse of a riddle-poem about something in the garden.[8]

> He is not John the gardener,
> And yet the whole day long
> Employs himself most usefully,
> The flower-beds among.

Using a slightly different teaching sequence, the child works out the most difficult word in the first line, "gardener," and then does word-building (changing the initial consonant) with "not." Then the child reads the first line through. The second line is again taught by beginning with "whole" and "long," and word-building is done with "and" and "long." The third and fourth lines are done in the same way, and then the child can read the whole verse straight through. (There is no writing of words in the air in this lesson.) Finally, the teacher reads the rest of the poem to the student, and shows him a picture of the mystery helper.

Again, we have some new words (including the ones built up on the blackboard), a bit of nature study, and possibly even a little moral idea about employing oneself usefully. And the opportunity to think by building words and maybe by trying to puzzle out what the thing in the garden could be. (Do you know? The poem is "A Friend in the Garden," by Mrs. Ewing.) [9]

On Teaching Vocabulary

How do you teach or learn new vocabulary—by endless drills, by writing out definitions?

A more effective way is to listen to those who use words powerfully, and to read what they have written—and though that road may end with books written for adults, it begins much earlier. If we had wanted to limit our children's literary menu to books using the easiest and most commonly used words, we wouldn't have read them *Winnie the Pooh*, Beatrix Potter ("'I am affronted,' said Mrs. Tabitha Twitchit"), William Steig, the Bible, Jacobs' *English Folk and Fairy Tales*, Lewis Carroll, or Graham Oakley. Or Melissa Wiley (see below).

When Lydia turned six, she decided to read *Anne of Green Gables* to herself. The motivation was that she found a small porcelain Anne doll at one yard sale, and then a copy of *Anne* at the next one. We already owned two copies, but she wanted this one for her own, to go with her doll. For about a week, she sat in my grandfather's little rocking chair with her doll beside her, and read it while her dad read the newspaper. It was way beyond her vocabulary and experience, and I didn't expect her to get past the first couple of pages—but she got through about eight chapters by herself, and let me read her the ninth. I figured she would just skip what she didn't understand, but she still managed to grasp a fair amount of the story, particularly about Anne's imaginary friends. Would she have been better off with an adapted version? Define "better off." (Lydia is now fourteen, and that experience is still very clear in her memory. She has forgotten things I read to her, but not that book.)

Vocabulary increases naturally as we read books that lead us gently through unfamiliar territory—like Melissa Wiley's *Martha* series, set in Scotland in the 1700's.[10] Again it was Lydia who asked to be read these books. She became acquainted with box bed, waulking wool, governess, kirk, peat, spindle, flax, loch, dustgown, Hogmanay, and pianoforte. When I asked her if those were hard words, she said, "Kids know *dust* and kids know *gown*, so you just put them together and make *dustgown*." What's a governess? "A lady who takes care of you." No problem.

On Narration and the Act of Knowing

> This amazing gift with which normal
> children are born is allowed to lie fallow in
> their education.[11]

Narration is a Charlotte Mason bugaboo for both children and parents.

A bugaboo is something that causes fear or distress out of proportion to its importance. Anne of Green Gables' bugaboo was geometry.

Charlotte Mason, in one of her slightly sarcastic moods, said that "everybody" agrees that reading lots of books is a good idea. And that "they" also say that narration, as they understand it, is just a natural thing, that there's nothing special about telling back a story, so there is also little educational value in it. We don't commend a physical education teacher for letting kids run on the playground.

> This is nothing new, you will say, and
> possibly no natural law in action appears
> extraordinarily new; we take flying already as
> a matter of course; but though there is
> nothing surprising in the action of natural
> laws, the results are exceedingly surprising,
> and to that test we willingly submit these
> methods.[12]

Mason agreed that lots of people read books. She agreed that narration, writing or telling back, is something that we can do without trying very hard. Listen to anyone talking to a friend on the phone, and it's "So she said to me, and then I said to her..." Even the teller does not get any particular value out of simply retelling what he has heard or seen. The value is not in the narration, it is in the material.

What is the right material for narration? It should concern "many things on which the mind of man reflects."[13] It should be in literary form. "Literary form" is another bugaboo, or at least a point of contention, but it means, partly, that we learn best when there's some meat in the sandwich and pickles on the side. Some people with active imaginations can make an entertaining story out of even a wallpaper sample book, as a certain Canadian comedy team once demonstrated. But a "smoke and water feast," as Charlotte Mason said, only goes so far. A quick walk around the block isn't an afternoon in the country, and aniseed drops aren't lunch.

This is an example of what Charlotte Mason called literary style. It's from Dallas Lore Sharp's book *Summer*, one of a series of four delightful natural history books (one for each season).[14]

> Once we had gained the peak [of Mount
> Hood in Oregon], we lay down behind a pile
> of sulphurous rock, out of the way of the
> cutting wind, and watched the steam float
> up from the crater, with the widest world in
> view that I ever turned my eyes upon.
> The draft pulled hard about the openings
> among the rock-piles, but hardest up a flue,
> or chimney, that was left in the edge of the
> crater-rim where parts of the rock had fallen
> away.
> As we lay at the side of this flue, we soon
> discovered that butterflies were hovering
> about us; no, not hovering, but flying swiftly
> up between the rocks from somewhere
> down the flue. I could scarcely believe my
> eyes. What could any living thing be doing
> here?—and of all things, butterflies? This
> was three or four thousand feet above the
> last vestige of vegetation, a mere point of
> volcanic rock (the jagged edge-piece of an
> old crater) wrapped in eternal ice and snow,
> with sulphurous gases pouring over it, and
> across it blowing a wind that would freeze as

soon as the sun was out of the sky.
But here were real butterflies. I caught two
or three of them and found them to be
vanessas (*Vanessa californica*), a close relative
of our mourning-cloak butterfly. They were
all of one species, apparently, but what were
they doing here?

Students' reading should have as much variety as Frances the Badger's school lunchbox: "jam in the morning, jam at noon" will not do.[15] But even then we do not fully know what we've read until our own minds have performed the act of knowing. A bite of sandwich doesn't stay in the mouth, it has to get chewed up and go somewhere. Narration is not spitting the story back out; it is more like sharing the enjoyment of the meal. It is retelling with understanding.

So why is narration a bugaboo?

Because it's hard work. Because we don't always know if we've picked the right book, or if we're reading too much at a time, or expecting too much back. Because, being a hundred years removed from Charlotte Mason's time, we wonder if we're doing it right. Sometimes even her own books contradict each other: read directly from the Bible before any pictures or amplification, or after? How do you get children interested? How do you know what the little remarks afterward are supposed to be? What if they continue to complain and say, "I don't know?" Or "why are we doing this?"

Maybe we can tell them that, at one time, reading and learning were almost synonymous, and sometimes reading to learn meant freedom or even outright rebellion. In some parts of the world, that's still true. And if we can both establish narration as a habit, incorporating the "sub-habits" of attention, observation, and imagination, and make the students our allies in this business of acquiring knowledge, we may find less resistance.

Teachability is often confused with
subservience.... On the contrary, teachability
is an extremely active virtue. No one is really
teachable who does not freely exercise his

76

power of independent judgment. (Mortimer J. Adler, *How to Read a Book*) [16]

From our family homeschooling annals:

Lydia and I sat down this morning to do Grade One. One day it's *Paddle-to-the-Sea*, another day it's a fairy tale or *Just-So Stories*. Usually we read something from *A Child's Garden of Verses* and either a fable or one of the *Fifty Famous Stories Retold* as well, since they're pretty short.

Today we were about to start "Alexander and Bucephalus" from *Fifty Famous Stories Retold*.[17] But first I asked her to go to the bookcase and pick out a book: Start in the middle. Now higher! To the right! Count five books over! What's the name of the book? *Stories of Alexander the Great*, by Pierre Grimal.[18] I love this book; oldest sister Josi and I read it in the backyard on a blanket, the summer Lydia was born.

"That's who this story is about," I said. "Alexander the Great."

"Then let's read it out of this book," Lydia said.

"Well...okay." So I read the story in Grimal's words, and Lydia started narrating it all back to me:

"Once upon a time there was a king who was going to buy a horse for a famous price. [She meant fabulous.] Famous price now means that it's cheap, but a famous price then meant it was really expensive."

Fifth-grader Audrey had wandered in after finishing her own assignment, and she said, "I remember this story. This is a good story."

Lydia by this time had really gotten into her narration.

"Alexander said, 'I can ride this horse.' His father the king made a deal with him. If he couldn't ride the horse, he would have to pay the whole price of the horse himself."

"Do you want a horse?" Audrey offered. "I'll be the horse."

Lydia considered the offer, and then took Audrey by the "bridle" and continued.

"He took the horse and turned him so he couldn't see his shadow. Then he got on and rode the horse. Then he galloped the horse."

(Audrey: "Ooh! Ow!" But she was a good sport.)

Lydia finished her narration, Audrey got up from her knees, and we decided that one story was about enough for Grade One today.

On Teaching Grammar

Charlotte Mason referred to Plato's idea that knowledge and virtue are fundamentally identical.[19] This could mean that that if you know something is right, then you must act on it; but also it also implies that there is a spiritual side to all knowledge. There is someone or something who gives us the ability to know, and the conviction that we *can* know.[20] Mason believed in the role of the Holy Spirit in learning—all kinds of learning, not only theological. Our feet are "set in a large room" when we recognize the relation of the Divine Teacher and the students, in things of the mind and the spirit.

She argued that if we present even a mundane subject like grammar honestly and correctly, making use of its simplest, most direct principles and its particular "guiding ideas," "without pedantry and without verbiage," then we could reasonably invoke the help of the Spirit in its teaching. And if not, we had better not.

What did she mean by that? A twenty-minute grammar lesson, written for upper elementary students, gives us an example.[21]

First, as in each of the *Parents' Review* "Notes of Lessons," we are given several objects: "to increase the children's power of reasoning and attention, to increase their knowledge of English Grammar, and to introduce a new part of speech—prepositions." So if we want not only to teach what prepositions are, but also to encourage reasoning and attention, what do we need to do?

First, we ask for something that the children have already learned: in this case, the difference between transitive and intransitive verbs, asking for examples to write on the blackboard. Intransitive verbs cannot have a direct object, so "Cerberus sleeps" is intransitive. (If you say "Cerberus sleeps in the underworld," you are jumping ahead; for now we will leave out the preposition and say that Cerberus cannot "sleep anything.")

Now the new material starts. The teacher gives the children something to think about: a sentence beginning "Odysseus went..." They are to make it more complete by adding an object. "Odysseus went Troy" does not make sense, but "Odysseus went to Troy" does. The teacher asks for other phrases to complete the sentence, hoping that the students will use different prepositions.

Then we have the explanation: "Tell the children that these little words on, in, by, for, with, etc., belong to a class of little words which are very much used with intransitive verbs, and though they have not much meaning when used alone, yet in a sentence they cannot stand without an object. You cannot say 'Odysseus went on' without saying what he went on." (This does not seem like too much "verbiage.")

The next step is to give the reason and memory-helper for the term preposition: prepositions go *before* the object, and "pre" means *before*. The teacher writes out the definition, "A preposition always has an object after it." (There is no explanation of direct and indirect objects; worrying about details that don't apply to this lesson would be pedantic.)

Finally, the children get to work through several exercises (it is not specified whether these are oral or written). The teacher gives a preposition (in, on, over, by, with, from), and the students supply three objects for each. They also fill in the blanks where the preposition is missing from a sentence (looking for more than one possibility for each), and where the subjects and verbs are missing instead. They make new sentences, using prompts such as "The white sails."

Note, again, that this is a lesson for upper elementary students. Primary students were transcribing sentences and writing from dictation, so they were certainly getting a sense of how words worked and where punctuation went; but they were not expected to be dealing with intransitive verbs. There is no section for Grammar on the primary-level examination papers.

A Book to be Loved

> Our earliest literature was history and
> poetry. Indeed, we might say poetry only,
> for in those far-off times history was always
> poetry, it being only through the songs of
> the bards and minstrels that history was
> known. And when I say history I do not
> mean history as we know it. It was then
> merely the gallant tale of some hero's deeds
> listened to because it was a gallant tale.
> (*English Literature for Boys and Girls*) [22]

Charlotte Mason's curriculum has always had a reputation for emphasizing "dusty old books," especially in literature, right from the time when the Parents' Union School first offered its programmes. Even in the work for the youngest ones, Mason refused to swerve from the classics, or from just about anything written after 1900.

The clue to this may be in a passage where she almost apologetically pointed out that the literature for the two highest forms (senior high school) was mostly older books—but that she assumed that the older students would have no trouble choosing their own reading from current literature. In other words, she expected that they *would* read outside of class, and that what they had read in school would give them the background to read critically and thoughtfully. The assumption is that we're still talking about quality literature, not throwaway novels; but the point is that Charlotte Mason wasn't excluding new books. But she was limiting the curriculum, perhaps, to books that students might not have picked up on their own.

The idea of English literature as an area of study was still very new in Mason's time; in fact, the earliest term programmes don't even have a "literature" heading, but list poetry and novels under "history." It was a bit ground-breaking to emphasize Scott's novels, Charles Kingsley, Tennyson's poems about King Arthur; and not just as pieces in school readers, but given whole, with appreciation and respect. Charlotte Mason must have been delighted to discover *English Literature for Boys and Girls*; it is a treasure trove of stories about the best English books and their authors, through the centuries.

> In Forms III and IV we introduce a History
> of English Literature carefully chosen to
> afford sympathetic interest and delight while
> avoiding stereotyped opinions and stale
> information. The portion read each term
> (say fifty pages) corresponds with the period
> covered in history studies and the book is a
> great favourite with children.[23]

Compare that to more recent books that tell only about writers and books specifically for children, and you hear a sound like doors closing. A couple of summers ago I was looking for English resources for my middle-schooler, and out of curiosity I downloaded some chapters from a current Language Arts textbook. What I liked about the book was that it had good assignments and asked some big questions, on heroism, the human family, peace. The problem was that the reading material included in the textbook wasn't equal to those questions. The students were being asked to think critically, but the content was an appetizer, not a feast. If you're going to ask the big questions, you had better let the seekers into the cave where they can at least start looking for the big answers.

A Literature Lesson

> A person who knows nothing about
> literature may be an ignoramus, but many
> people don't mind being that. Every child
> realizes that literature is taking him in a
> different direction from the immediately
> useful, and a good many children complain
> loudly about this. (Northrop Frye, *The
> Educated Imagination*) [24]

And why, again, are we emphasizing literature? To what end? We don't read Shakespeare with children by giving them long vocabulary lists on which to be quizzed; in fact, we don't read it with them to enrich their vocabularies, or to teach them about Julius Caesar or what blank verse is. We definitely don't read it because we want to show off what homeschools or private schools can do. We read it with them because we want to give them something that already belongs to them. We read it, as we look at paintings and stars and cathedrals, to gain some lasting "mind furniture." We read it because it's beautiful and true, because it helps us to understand God and people. We read it to go beyond ourselves.

> In most other school subjects, what is
> chiefly needed for success is hard work, as
> little emotional as possible, but in literature,
> the love for the subject is the measure of the
> good to be got from it, and a proper manual
> for pupils ought to be a book to be loved,
> not a treatise to be crammed. [25]

How do you properly give a lesson in literature, since it is not chemistry, grammar, or algebra? As explained in a *Parents' Review* article by S. De Brath, let's say we are introducing an English ballad such as "Chevy Chase" to a group of twelve-year-olds, and we have forty-five minutes. [26] That might sound like much too long a time to teach one poem, but we want to give this ballad its due, and help the students to really hear it, not just read it casually. So we might begin with a picture that has something in it the students will recognize; or we could refer back to another lesson, mentioning something from the same time period. Using the example of "Chevy Chase," our author suggests that we refer back to geography lessons on the Scottish Border, since the ballad is about a hunting party that accidentally ends up in a border skirmish. De Brath also suggests a brief description of fourteenth-century castles and weapons, to help everyone imagine the setting.

> *Lo, yonder doth Earl Douglas come*
> *His men in armour bright*
> *Full twenty hundred Scottish spears*
> *All marching in our sight.*

> *Show me, said he, whose men you be*
> *That hunt so boldly here*
> *That, without my consent do chase*
> *And kill my fallow deer?*

Whatever we choose, it should focus everyone's attention on the subject, link the known to the unknown, and remind the teacher of what the students already know. This introduction might take fifteen minutes.

The actual reading of the poem, in this case, is allowed twenty minutes. Then De Brath says that, in the last ten minutes,

> The Literature lesson should not conclude
> with a dry resume of the action in bald
> prose, but it may be well to bring out what
> has specially appealed to different children.
> This should be a most valuable lesson to the
> teacher, who can thus get a glimpse into the
> minds of his class which work far more
> definitely than, as a rule, he has any idea of.

> *Their bodies bathed in purple gore*
> *They bore with them away;*
> *They kissed their dead a thousand times*
> *When they were clad in clay.*

God save our king, and bless this land
With plenty, joy and peace,
And grant henceforth that foule debate
'Twixt noblemen may cease! [27]

Chapter 7:   Get Some Grit

Oh dear, when shall we learn not to take
ourselves and other people as inevitable!
Don't you see, the faults are in the child's
bringing-up, not in her disposition. It is to
her bringing-up she owes the refinement and
intelligence you notice; and it is to her
bringing-up she owes the disappointing fact
that she continually falls into the ranks of
girls younger and more ignorant than
herself. It is impossible to pull her up. She
will be at a disadvantage all her school-life.
She will get into the habit of being at a
disadvantage, and will not have the
necessary self-confidence to take her fit
place in the world. It is all summed up in a
word; she has been brought up at home.[1]

Did Charlotte Mason really say that homeschoolers are at a
disadvantage? Lacking good study habits? Badly brought up? And we
thought she was our friend.

Is it a necessary evil that homeschooled students do not work as
hard as they might? No, and that was Mason's point. She thought

that potential problems could be avoided by giving parents a stronger education plan (including early emphasis on habit training, and later an understanding of the Will), and giving children (and parents) a stronger connection with others who were doing the same work. When I first started homeschooling, most people didn't have Internet connections; we were lucky to have a good local support group. I noticed, over those first few years, that when I heard of people who had tried homeschooling but gave up after a short time, it was almost always because they tried to do it all on their own. Those who had even a few more experienced friends to call on for help seemed more likely to persevere.

Many homeschoolers now are not in the least isolated, with the many community and other activities that they take part in. But when it comes to academic work and personal discipline, we still need to make sure that our young students are taught to care about their work, to take learning seriously. Not for spelling bees, not for college, and not because they are trying to make us happy; but because education is about knowledge for its own sake, and finding our connections on this planet and in this universe.

Parenting with Grit

In 1891, a *Parents' Review* article by "Mrs. Ward" discussed what was wrong with ways of raising children in years gone by (strict and stern, repressive, tyrannical) and with the then-current parental attitudes (too lenient in some ways, too smothering in others).

> We not infrequently hear that children now
> tend to grow up nerveless and unenergetic
> and self-indulgent; that they face no
> difficulties, endure nothing quietly, exert no
> original force. They have no idea of "striving
> to attain," and become disgusted and
> miserable when the good things of life are
> not found all ready to their hand; they have
> no ideals or strong interests of any kind, and
> lack the power as well as the will to help
> themselves. While expecting to be provided
> with many means of happiness, they are

unable to make good use of them, because
they lack the energy and the eagerness which
alone make continued enjoyment possible.[2]

Mrs Ward talked about Froebel's theory that children should be protected from as much harshness as possible; and Locke's advice that "children should occasionally be put to some pain to accustom them to bear it," using these as examples of parenting extremes from the past. Then she said, "Let us wait a bit, however, and we shall find the next generation taking its turn to pick holes."

What is it that we want young adults to be or to have? What is it that they want to be? Mrs. Ward listed "energy, self-reliance, self-control, endurance, and dignity—of everything, in fact, that is commonly summed up under the phrase 'strength of character,' or in the Scotch term 'grit.'" I remember learning in psychology class about the different stages of internal conflict we experience as we grow: feeling frustration as children because (like it or not) we feel weak and helpless, and we wish we were bigger, stronger, more capable. If we didn't feel at least some dissatisfaction with being a child, we wouldn't have the motivation to mature. But it seems to me that if children grow up knowing that they *are* able to have energy, *can* show self-reliance, *ought* to have self-control, and have the *will* to endure, they may miss out on some of that frustration. And that's not a bad thing.

Let's turn the list of complaints around. Young adults with "grit" should be the opposite of "nerveless and unenergetic." They should be the doers, the workers, the ones who go and get the leaf blower without being asked, and not because the tree boss is standing over them. If they are not self-indulgent, they should be able to control their own desires, and to put other needs or work first. They should be able to face difficulties, endure many things quietly, and "exert original force," that is, take initiative, accept the things they can't change, but change the things they can. They need to "strive to attain," not to compete with others, but to do their own best at something. They should have ideals and strong interests, things they care about. They need to find happiness that is within themselves (not dependent on others or on material possessions) but is also outwardly focused. Is anyone going to argue with that?

But where does grit, "menschliness," or character come from?

The Skill to Turn the Key

[Attention] is the power of bending such
powers as one has to the work in hand; it is
a key to success within the reach of every
one, but the skill to turn it comes of training.
Circumstances may compel a man to train
himself, but he does so at the cost of great
effort, and the chances are ten to one against
his making the effort. For the child, on the
other hand, who has been trained by his
parents to fix his thoughts, all is plain sailing.
He will succeed, not a doubt of it.[3]

Here is the problem: although teenagers and even adults can learn and change for the better, this training in Will should begin much, much earlier. Have you ever seen a parent and small child interacting and thought, "Trouble, there, in a few years?"

Charlotte Mason said that parents need to be clear with children about who's accountable to whom.[4] Children have to answer to their parents, but parents have to answer to God, and they are required to both care for children's needs and "train them in the way they should go." Mason pointed out the difference between two possibly unpopular parental decisions. The first is making an inactive or indoors-preferring child go out and get the fresh air and exercise she needs. The parent knows that she is doing right by the child, even if the easier way would be to let him stay inside. The other situation is an unsociable parent who refuses to let older children have normal friendships and activities. In that case, he is exercising parental authority, but for selfish, personal reasons.

That doesn't mean that every household rule has to be posted on the wall, or that a parent can't be flexible as long as a principle isn't being violated. But bullying, guilt-tripping, and manipulation are forbidden for both parents and children. Don't wheedle and cajole children into doing things, but don't let them wheedle and cajole you either. And it's not all about constant and unquestioning obedience; at least, not when that training later hinders us from acting with intelligence and courage. Mrs. Ward said that, like seed without deep roots, unthinking or fear-based good conduct does not enable us to make real choices. If home or school has felt like a prison, full of arbitrary rules, without happiness or freedom, that makes it even worse. We want to escape, but in the meantime we learn not to care too much about anything. Bitter and rebellious attitudes are not the fruit of a strong character tree.

How Hard Should Life Be?

> No endeavour to strengthen a child's will
> and to create self-reliance, energy, and
> endurance, will succeed if his life be dull and
> dreary... Having few things presented to
> them worth caring for or struggling for, they
> grow up apathetic and indolent.[5]

There are places and times where life is harsh, where even basic existence is a struggle, and caring about beauty in the home or providing playthings for children requires more energy than seems possible. There is a huge need in the world for menders, healers, encouragers.

However, most of us live in more secure environments, and the problem now is often one of many things instead of few. We need to teach our children to appreciate and take care of special toys (and make things for themselves or for others). Not everything *should* be easy; everyone needs to learn to do a job properly, even when nobody's looking. It doesn't hurt to learn to wait for things. But letting children know they're loved and safe isn't spoiling them.

In another *Parents' Review* article, "Early Tendencies in the Child" by Mrs. Sieveking, I notice two things.[6] One is a continual return to the big picture; how a positive adult outlook comes out of early love and good teaching. The other is the idea that parental action is not all about scoldings, discipline, and reining in the youngsters; it's also about the wholesome things that we do provide. A more current phrase might be "healthy alternatives." This means true parental involvement! Not materialistic spoiling or pandering, but an adult who pays serious attention to a child's artistic efforts; taking him along on errands (particular those that offer the chance to spend some time outdoors together); encouraging interests and hobbies; talking and listening. Mrs. Sieveking suggested that removing children from negative situations—for instance, getting them outdoors, away from electronic screens—would offer a natural and non-patronizing way to work out some of their knots. Working outdoors together might be a more motivating way to combat lazy tendencies than by scolding, or forcing children to do extra chores indoors.

It all takes time. Time together. Time that most people don't have. Not time to chauffeur the kids to more structured activities, but to go out and look at things together; to have occasional surprises and adventures; to find shared interests; to store up special memories.

> ...this way delight is necessary for happiness.
> For it is caused by the appetite being at rest
> in the good attained. (St. Thomas Aquinas) [7]

Applying This Chapter with Younger Students

Children should be allowed to work towards things they want, rather than having everything given to them. The same system of natural rewards can apply during school lessons; if assignments are done well and with time to spare, that time should be the students'. They should have a right to their own property, including personal books and toys, and should be responsible for taking care of their things. (Parents may have to ensure that smaller people don't get into what doesn't belong to them.)

Children should be expected to do their schoolwork and chores energetically and to the best of their abilities. Even a small child can be proud of having done a good job, and sticking with something until it's done.

They should also be held responsible for hurting someone or damaging property. It is not harmful for a child to have to work off the price of repairs by helping fix the damage or giving back in some other way. Insistence on exact reparations can sometimes backfire, as in the case of a boy in our first-grade class who was ordered to sew up—badly and awkwardly—a girl's sweater that he had torn. There are cases where it may be more prudent to protect the victim (or her property) from further damage! There are also times when the damage or injury is large and serious, not within the child's capacity to mend or pay for, but he should still understand his responsibility and do what he can.

Applying This Chapter with Older Students

An old but still useful book that illustrates the value of self-reliance is *Meet the Malones*, the first book in the *Beany Malone* series.[8] Set during the Second World War, it introduces the four Malone offspring who are known for their generosity and sense of responsibility. That doesn't mean they don't make mistakes: one of the girls puts a down payment on an old horse, and her brother smashes his jalopy into a truck full of eggs and has to pay off the damage (and buy the eggs). Their journalist father goes off on assignment and sends them three war orphans, and the married sister arrives with a new baby when her husband is sent overseas. (At least they have eggs to eat.) Into all this arrives a domineering grandmother who pays off the debts and buys them their hearts' deepest desires, resulting in crushed spirits and the disappearance of the horse. When Grandma attempts to get rid of the orphans as well, the Malones realize that things have gone too far and that they have to find their "grit" again.

But there are many other books that also illustrate "energy, self-reliance, self-control, endurance, and dignity." Not about perfect people, necessarily, but those with grit.

Minds More Awake

Chapter 8: The Unconscious Constant Factor (Mathematics)

There is nothing in arithmetic that need prove an undue tax on the powers of any average child, were not the real difficulties complicated by being entangled with others which are imaginative, or one might almost say moral.

Many children, clever at actual calculations, fail miserably in algebra examinations (and in many more important crises of life), for lack of agility in detecting what is, and what is not, relevant to the special point under consideration. (Mary Everest Boole)[1]

Mathematician Mary Everest Boole was a regular early contributor to Charlotte Mason's *Parents' Review* magazine, and several of her articles on mathematics and science are available on the AmblesideOnline website (and well worth reading).[2]

A recent lesson in my eighth grader's math book showed the difference between a circle and an ellipse, demonstrating that an ellipse has two foci, and that the sum of the distances between any point on the ellipse and the foci will be same as the sum of the distances between any other point and the foci. She was to put a piece of paper on some corrugated cardboard, and draw an ellipse, using two tacks and a piece of string as an improvised compass. The book also had a drawing of planets following elliptical orbits.[3]

In Boole's article "Home Algebra and Geometry," I found this:

> Explain that an ellipse is (not exactly the
> path of any planet, but) the one among the
> simpler curves which is most like a planet
> path, and therefore important to understand.
> Then, shew that we cannot draw an ellipse
> without putting two pins in the two foci; yet
> nature makes the planet go round with only
> one sun in focus, the other being left empty.
> This is an excellent typical instance of the
> relation between nature's facts and our
> devices for analyzing those facts.
> Set the child to draw ellipses with the pins
> nearer and nearer together, till they come
> into one hole; then with the pins further and
> further apart. Tell him that the resulting
> circle and straight line are called the limiting
> forms of the ellipse...
> Shew that, though the distance of the pencil
> from any one focus is constantly varying, yet
> the sum of the distances from the two foci is
> always the same in the same ellipse.[4]

And there's more: the lesson (which may go on over a period of time) takes in slingshot stones, gravitational pull, and glimmerings of calculus. This is not baby math by any means, although it's what Boole called "play-lessons," or "holiday lessons." We could call it "math club." Something perhaps outside of the normal stream of formal math lessons, but "fruitful for future development." It is all very big-picture and principle-driven. Yet it starts by drawing ellipses with a string and two tacks. (Mary Everest Boole also gets credit for inspiring String Art.)

She also pointed out that if a child plays with a yo-yo (she calls it a Bandelore), he might notice that the disk stops briefly at the top and at the bottom, which is the basis of understanding maxima and minima, or limits, in calculus. When he eventually works with equations, he will have that mental image to illustrate what might otherwise seem like pointless math-class torture. In Augustinian terms, he sees the thing and knows it before he has to name it or formally describe it.

Boole explained this division between "play" and "work" math:

> Every child's mind is in direct contact with
> abstract Truth, and can imbibe it by the
> natural use of its own powers...The Truth-
> absorption is the proper business of Holy-
> days, of quiet leisurely hours free from the
> stress of work.
>
> Work is connected with and regulated by
> our relation to Humanity, our duties as
> citizens, and should be done in the most
> orderly and convenient way possible,
> irrespective of any special manner in which
> Abstract Truth may have revealed itself to
> the individual. ("Home Arithmetic") [5]

In other words, there is a time to experiment, and a time to just do what you're supposed to do. Both are necessary for learning.

For younger children, she also recommended "play lessons" as a way to let them experience arithmetic operations with concrete or discovery activities, before they are expected to deal with them in more conventional ways. A child might be doing paper-and-pencil addition and subtraction during arithmetic lessons, but could also be learning early multiplication concepts by building her own multiplication table and experimenting with its uses. Even before that, according to Boole, children can start learning place value by playing trading games with pennies and dimes, or with two colours of counters. Then you (the teacher) move on to teaching addition with the same coins or counters, using written numerals but without fussing over whether he begins adding with the tens or the units.

> When he can do an easy addition, of about three
> columns and three rows, slowly, but without effort,

beginning indifferently at either end, and can explain the rationale of each process, addition may pass to the stage of "work." Subtraction should then be taken up for play-lesson, the same principle being observed as in play addition.

> Point out that, though we perform our investigations on fragments of a large number, because, our faculties being limited, we cannot multiply it as a whole, yet we write the word "Answer" opposite to no partial result, but only to that expression which indicates the summary or synthesis of our various partial investigations. This forms a good preparation for understanding that doctrine, which is at once the basis of Mathematical Philosophy and its crowning glory; viz: the doctrine that man is related by his analytic faculties to the monkeys who investigate by breaking things in pieces, and, by his synthetic faculty, to that Unity in Whom are reunited all that has been separated...

Here are some other math concepts that Boole said children should learn informally:

1. Knowing that there are different but still correct ways to express equivalent amounts of things, including parts of things, remainders, change. We can say a month and a half, or six weeks. Half-past three is the same as 3:30 (or maybe 15:30). The doll might be a foot and a half tall, but she is also eighteen inches. The words used to express size or amount don't change the nature of the object.

> Nothing in mathematical philosophy is more beautiful than the way in which a set of equivalent arithmetical expressions reflect various possible conceptions of the same

action; every child should be free to soak in this marvel, in silence and at his own pace. But he cannot do that while some one is explaining "divisions of money" to him; if he is confronted with the spiritual revelation and the intellectual problem at the same moment, he will miss the enjoyment of the one, and his facility in mastering the other will suffer also...

2. The hard-to-understand concept of cutting things into pieces and getting a larger number than you had before. Why do six half-cookies become three wholes when you put them together, not losing any cookie along the way? Or you can demonstrate the magic of breaking one cookie in half and getting two—but it doesn't take long until they notice the problem with that. Another difficulty with fractions is understanding that a third is more than a fourth, which is more than a tenth or a hundredth. (Words like half or quarter will not be as obvious, unless you are writing them out.)

> Two little cooks...have found five eggs. Minnie shall make a pudding with two to-day, and Beckey shall use two to-morrow in a cake. But what shall we do with the fifth egg? We might break it to-day and divide it in two, and each child would then have two eggs and a half. But it would be inconvenient and messy; we had better leave one egg "over."

> Finally, a single lily bulb may be given to two children, with the suggestion that it is to be shared between them. They may thus be led to see that a live thing cannot be divided; the only thing that can be shared is the pleasure of watching it grow—a possession which is

not diminished by being enjoyed by more
than one person participating in it.
("Nursery Examples of Fractions")

3. We should sometimes ask children questions like this: "If each child can get six walnuts out of a bag by dipping with his hands, how many will be got out by four children? Three children? Two children? One child? Half a child?" They will think the inclusion of "half a child" is funny, but introducing the possibility of "less than one" is good practice in reasoning.

4. We can sometimes ask a question that involves a mixture of the solvable and the unsolvable. "If there are six children, one dog, and two cans of paint in the backyard, how many feet are there? How many eyes? How many t-shirts? How much trouble can they get into?"

Is this math? You might say it's more just common sense. However, Boole explained:

> What we need to produce, in relation to
> such a matter, is not intellectual conviction,
> but a vivid and abiding mental picture, an
> "unconscious constant factor" in the mind, a
> crystallizing thread round which future
> wisdom may gather and organize itself.

Like nature study, like reading lessons, like picture talks, what the young child is doing is collecting "mental pictures," "crystallizing threads." (Herbartian teachers would say he is building up his apperception masses.) This is not just for preschool children, but all along the way as preparation for new levels of work. In any new area of study, there is a sort of "play" that should happen first, a time of observation and of free exploration, which (Boole said) is also the time when we may discover important ideas. Once we start in on long division, we won't have much extra time to muse on what it actually means.

Boole ended with a most important question:

> "What advantage will come to each of two persons, when each receives half of what was a living healthy bulb weighing five ounces?" Answer:—"Each will receive two and a half ounces of useless, dying vegetable material." The mother who has furnished her children's mind-chambers with clear images of the various kinds of halving, will have done more to facilitate their future study of fractions than she could have done by any amount of premature explanation of numerical processes.

Lost Treasures of Charlotte Mason, #3

Ourselves *(Book I), Part III, Chapters 1-4*

> All the great possibilities of Love are in
> every human heart, and to touch the spring,
> one must give Love.

But not love that demands and has to have; this is a love that serves, that goes beyond self, in small things as well as great.

> [Love] shrinks from causing uneasiness to
> his friend by fretful or sullen tempers,
> jealousy or mistrust.

No jealousy? No mistrust? No sulking?

> Still more careful must we be never to go
> over in our minds for an instant any chance,
> hasty, or even intended word or look that
> might offend us...Never let us think over our
> small pains, and our great pains will be easily
> endurable.

It's not that you don't have a right to be irritated; it's that you have better things to think about. Imagine how much interpersonal drama that kind of thinking would eliminate.

One of the "better things to think about" is compassion for others. In Louisa May Alcott's novel *Jack and Jill*, both of the title characters are hurt in a sledding accident, and are stuck in bed in their own homes, next door to each other. Someone rigs up a clothesline and a basket between the bedroom windows, and the two patients forget their own troubles while thinking of jokes and gifts to send each other over the clothesline.[1]

> Be quick to discern their pains and
> sufferings, and be ready to bring help...if our
> minds are occupied with others, far and
> near, at home and abroad, we shall have

neither time nor inclination to be sorry for
ourselves.

But what about one we don't love, or, more typically, don't hate,
but don't like because we don't understand him? Charlotte Mason
said that the way to get over the dislike caused by not knowing
someone is to "try to realise him from his own point of view."

One summer I worked at a camp for adults with intellectual
disabilities. I had recently been to a yard sale and had picked up some
vintage band records, along with a record player. One hot evening I
plugged it in and tried out the records. When I put on one tune from
the 1930's, an older guest who was usually very crotchety and
withdrawn suddenly got excited and vocal. He started telling us how
they played that song at dances years ago, and how he and his brother
drove around together in a Model T Ford and provided music for
parties. I think it was the most any of us had ever heard him say, and
it revealed him as a whole person with a story.

> If music, poetry, art, give us joy, let us not
> hesitate to present these joys to others; for,
> indeed, those others are all made in all
> points like as we are, though with a different
> experience.[2]

Chapter 9: Global Vision

...reforming his life by virtue and learning,
and knowing God thereby (the best example
that can be possible, and by whom all the
whole world is ruled and governed, which
otherwise were out of all order and
confused)... (Plutarch's "Life of Dion")[1]

The first time my oldest daughter and I read Plutarch, she would have been almost ten. We jumped into the "Life of Demosthenes," without paddles or life jackets, and almost without a boat. I don't remember if we stuck with it for the whole term or just gave up.

However, Charlotte Mason said that Plutarch was important, and I trusted her judgement. We had managed Shakespeare, even some Beowulf, so this one would not defeat us. I decided that for the next term I would be better prepared.

Mason wrote that children couldn't get enough of Publicola, so that is where I started. I thought I knew some history, but I didn't know Publicola; I didn't know what a consul was; I was even vague on the difference between the Roman Republic and the Empire. Still, I had the whole summer before the next term started, so I printed out and read through Plutarch's "Life of Publicola."[2] I read it again. Then I read it again. I wrote down questions, circled words, and underlined place names. The story of Rome and its founding fathers started to make sense to me; but would my ten-year-old get anything out of it? Could I use what I had found out to smooth the way, but still not give her too much, and allow her to dig a bit for answers?

It seemed to work, and Publicola went much more smoothly than Demosthenes (we revisited him later). That set of notes became the introduction to Plutarch for all three of my daughters, and others who have used it through the AmblesideOnline curriculum.[3] The girls don't remember all the Plutarch we read; but they all remember the plot against Brutus, how a slave overheard the whole thing and risked his life to save the consul. They also remember Publicola tearing down his house so that his integrity would not be questioned.

> And to say truly, Valerius [Publicola] dwelt
> in a house a little too sumptuously built and
> seated, upon the hanging of the hill called
> Mount Velia: and because it stood high, it
> overlooked all the marketplace, so that any
> man might easily see from thence what was
> done there....when he came out of his house,
> it was a marvelous pomp and state to see
> him come down from so high a place, and
> with a train after him, that carried the
> majesty of a King's court.
>
> But herein Valerius left a noble example,
> shewing how much it importeth a noble
> man and magistrate, to have his ears open to
> hear, and willingly to receive free speech
> instead of flatteries, and plain truth in place
> of lies. For, being informed by some of his
> friends how the people misliked and
> complained of it, he stood not in his own
> conceit, neither was angry with them : but
> forthwith set workmen upon it, early in the
> morning before break of day, and
> commanded them to pluck down his house,
> and to raze it to the ground. Insomuch as
> the next day following, when the Romans

were gathered together in the marketplace, and saw this great sudden ruin, they much commended the noble act and mind of Valerius, in doing that he did : but so were they angry, and sorry both, to see so fair and stately a built house (which was an ornament to the city) overthrown upon a sudden... For his friends received him into their houses, until such time as the people had given him a place, where they did build him a new house, far more orderly, and nothing so stately and curious as the first was, and it was in the same place, where the temple called Vicus standeth at this day. ("Life of Publicola," Thomas North's translation) [4]

Over the years, we trotted back and forth between Republican consuls, Syracusan tyrants, and Macedonian kings. We compared Plutarch's Coriolanus with Shakespeare's adaptation of the story (a lesson in the art of play writing). (We mostly used Dryden's translation, to start with, although more recently we have taken on North's.)

Why Plutarch?

The decision to include Plutarch's *Lives*—or not—or in what translation—becomes a kind of touchpoint for how we view (or do) a Charlotte Mason education. Shakespeare is easy; everyone knows Shakespeare, recognizes Shakespeare. Nobody argues with teaching Shakespeare. But Plutarch belongs much more unmistakably to Charlotte Mason. If homeschooling was the world and Charlotte Mason was Canada, Plutarch would be maple syrup. We need to ask, and it's a fair question, if this was just one of those quaint turn-of-the-century ideas, like making Smyrna rugs for handicrafts; if Plutarch's *Lives* is essential in itself, or if what it offers could much more easily be acquired through newer books. Why did Charlotte Mason include this particular piece of antiquity?

Here are some of the reasons that Mason gave herself, or that were noted by her colleagues:

1) In the preface to Ourselves, she wrote that the novels of Sir Walter Scott and Plutarch's Lives were "sources that fall within everybody's reading." Obviously, this is not the case now, but at one time, Plutarch was considered common currency. Shakespeare read Plutarch. Abraham Lincoln read Plutarch. Frankenstein's monster read Plutarch. Ralph Waldo Emerson begins his essay on Plutarch with the words, "It is remarkable that of an author so familiar as Plutarch, not only to scholars, but to all reading men..."[5] Plutarch is not studied in most contemporary schools, at least below university level, but he was less obscure in previous eras than we may realize.

2) Similarly, the introduction of Plutarch at what seems a younger-than-necessary age was explained in *Parents and Children*[6] as part of a plan that brings a child to the world's library door, and offers him the key to its contents. (It is worth noting that Mason mentions only two books in that passage: *Tanglewood Tales*[7] for young children, and then Plutarch's *Lives*.) We don't just hand the child these books; we read them to him, but without too much explanation, a gift from one book-loving friend to another. We read, he narrates, we discuss, but we do not limit what he learns to our own ideas about it. My own prepared notes might seem to be at cross-purposes with Mason's "pick it up and read" attitude, but I justify them with the hope that they will encourage those of us (including myself) who did not grow up with Plutarch. (As Charlotte mentioned, though, some of the stories Plutarch tells are not suitable for young ears, or even sensitive adult ones. Pre-reading is strongly recommended.)

3) As well as an early beginning to literature and the habit of reading in general, Plutarch offers "the best preparation for the study of Grecian or of Roman history."[8] Note that Mason said preparation for history, not history itself. It is a familiarizing, a paving of the way. After reading several of Plutarch's *Lives*, we begin to recognize not only the characters, but common events such as the annual election of Roman consuls. We remember the fact that Corinth founded the colony of Syracuse in Sicily, and so it was natural for Syracuse to ask Corinth for help when it was

being attacked by Carthage.[9] Why was it so easy for Carthage to attack? We look at the map and see that Africa is just a short hop over the Mediterranean from Sicily. (Geography slips in there too.)

4) The book *In Memoriam* says that Charlotte Mason lived during an age that was fascinated by history, but that her "standards of judgement were ethical" and that "greatness in goodness was her ideal."[10] The characters profiled by Plutarch illustrate the best and worst of the Will: serving yourself, serving others, citizenship, leadership, service, kingdoms, power, greed, government, laws, the ideas that shape our lives, how people act on those ideas, and the consequences. Miss Ambler, the author of a *Parents' Review* article on teaching Plutarch, agreed:

> We need, however, to have more than a goal
> in view; we need to know the way to reach
> it. We know what is necessary for a good
> citizen, and we wish to send the children out
> equipped for service with high ideals and the
> courage to live up to them.[11]

We are offering not only keys to the love of books, to literature and history, but to children's own "Mansouls" (their inner beings).

The Subject of Citizenship

> To Study Citizenship is a Duty...
> Unfortunately so many people to-day are
> listless and ignorant and therefore
> unsuccessful in this important matter.
> Although citizens by right of birth they do
> not value their citizenship even enough to
> understand it. They accept all the benefits it
> brings them as a matter of course, but never
> trouble to ask the 'why' and the 'how' about
> them...Another powerful reason why all
> should study this subject is this: it may be

necessary one day to defend the privileges of
our full citizenship from those who would
take them from us and destroy them. (F.R.
Worts, *Citizenship*, 1919) [12]

Citizenship, at the time that Worts wrote his book, had become a
definite subject in Charlotte Mason's schools. It included studies in
leadership (such as Plutarch), civics topics, and "everyday morals,"
based on Mason's book *Ourselves*. AmblesideOnline continues to use
both Plutarch's *Lives* and *Ourselves*, which illustrates many of Mason's
beliefs about character development.

What about the rest, beyond the basic facts about voting and
charters of rights that you would need to know to pass a citizenship
test? Unfortunately, that's the really important stuff, and it's the part
for which the answers aren't as simple. What do young people need
to know to be citizens of their countries, to protect the freedoms and
rights they are promised, to carry out their own responsibilities, and
to be loyal, while still thinking for themselves?

In her *Parents' Review* article on Plutarch, Miss Ambler referred to a
passage on education for leadership, in Plutarch's "Life of
Dion." Dion is an uncle-by-marriage to young King Dionysius, who
has been raised to think only of his own entertainment, and who is
sadly lacking in kingdom-management skills.

> Dion therefore seeing (as we have said) the
> younger Dionysius clean marred, and in
> manner cast away for lack of good
> education, persuaded him the best he could
> to give himself unto study, and by the
> greatest entreaty he could possibly make, to
> pray the prince of all philosophers [Plato] to
> come into Sicily. And then when through his
> entreaty he were come, that he would refer
> himself wholly unto him, to the end that
> reforming his life by virtue and learning, and
> knowing God thereby (the best example that
> can be possible, and by whom all the whole
> world is ruled and governed, which

> otherwise were out of all order and
> confused), he should first obtain great
> happiness to himself, and consequently unto
> all his citizens also, who ever after through
> the temperance and justice of a father,
> would with goodwill do those things, which
> they presently unwillingly did for the fear of
> a lord, and in doing this, from a tyrant he
> should come to be a king. (Plutarch's "Life
> of Dion," Thomas North's translation)[13]

According to Plutarch, Dionysius needed to awaken his mind, to learn. He needed temperance, justice, and virtue, so that he could model these things for his subjects and treat them better. If he did this, Dion promised, the people would obey willingly, out of respect and not out of fear. Where was he supposed to learn all this? By studying with Plato.

> "It's all in Plato, all in Plato. Bless me, what
> do they teach them at these schools?" (C.S.
> Lewis, *The Last Battle*) [14]

Citizenship Isn't About Geography, Or Maybe It Is

> ...always beginning with the notion of an
> explorer who finds the land and measures
> it...[15]

Charlotte Mason said geography was something that would furnish the imagination. Do you remember George Bailey, the hero of *It's a Wonderful Life*? [16] When he was a boy, coconut wasn't just something to put on ice cream; it was a faraway place brought home. Ironically, coconut, or cocoa, or coffee, or cotton, may symbolize other countries just as much for us now, but in a negative way. Recently The Canadian Fair Trade Network and ReThink Communications launched an advertising campaign called "The Label Doesn't Tell the Whole Story."[17] That idea is something Charlotte Mason might have appreciated: looking beyond a sweater to the story (and struggles) of the person who made it. In a more positive way, stores such as Ten Thousand Villages add tags that tell how the person or co-operative that made a gift item benefits from its purchase.[18] Considering the food, clothing, and other products we buy is one way to start learning, and caring, about people who share our planet, and the places where they live.

> What they want, is, to have their eyes
> opened that they may see the rights of
> others as clearly as their own; and their
> reason cultivated, that they may have power
> to weigh the one against the other...[19]

Or Is It About History?

History was not meant to be interminable, but inexhaustible: a cave of knowledge treasures that could keep us collecting forever. With minds more awake, we are searching not for bare facts, but for principles. Examples of wisdom, or maybe of mistakes we don't want to repeat. "Imagination will bestir itself," Mason repeated, and "opinions come as knowledge grows."[20]

A somewhat unusual ninth-grade history lesson appeared in the *Parents' Review*, about then-current British political and economic issues.[21] The topics were the repeal of long-standing free trade laws and the involvement of Joseph Chamberlain (father of Neville Chamberlain) in the campaign to bring in a Preferential Tariff. Does all that sound fascinating? Maybe not, but as the author of the lesson pointed out, "it may be a turning point in our history." She had the students list the main points of the new policy, possible consequences of the tariff, the objections made by others, and Chamberlain's response. She mentioned several times that she wanted to draw these facts from the girls' own knowledge; the assumption was that they had been following these nationally important events in the newspaper and were capable of discussing them intelligently.

What stories are our students following? Do we regularly take time to organize the information, talk about the major players, ask how these events will benefit or hurt particular groups of people?

Or Nature Study? Science?

> Nature...gives us certain dispositions of mind which we can get from no other source, and it is through these right dispositions that we get life into focus, as it were; learn to distinguish between small matters and great, to see that we ourselves are not of very great importance, that the world is wide, that things are sweet, that people are sweet, too; that indeed, we are compassed about by an atmosphere of sweetness, airs of heaven coming from our God...we become prepared by the quiet schooling of nature to walk softly and do our duty towards man and towards God. [22]

> The rash conclusions and reckless statements of the person who has had no scientific training make him mischievous in society—a source of superstition and prejudice.[23]

What is Global Vision?

Recently I read *Not for Profit: Why Democracy Needs the Humanities*, by University of Chicago law and ethics professor Martha C. Nussbaum.[24] Nussbaum says that factual knowledge and logic alone are not enough to create a healthy civilization; we require "the narrative imagination," which includes an awareness of history. Without it, our over-confidence in technology threatens to turn us into "compliant machines."

Nussbaum's and Mason's ideas on educational reform do not run along all the same tracks. However, they agree on the need for education that recognizes human values, and on the consequences if it is lost. Charlotte Mason warned against utilitarian education.[25] Nussbaum warns against allowing education to be controlled by values of materialism and motives of short term profit, with an emphasis on science and technology but at the expense of the arts and humanities. An education that gives us a "mind more awake" does not concern itself primarily with careers, competition, and power. It is an agreement that life is about something larger. But how does government education reflect one set of beliefs or another? What about home education? Are we here to serve the system, or to serve God and people-kind?

This is not just a matter of taste, a choice about whether you buy tickets to a symphony concert or a hockey game. Utilitarian education does more than just ignore literature and history, art and music: it doesn't want them around at all. Nussbaum explains that

> The arts ask the imagination to see the world
> in new ways, so they are not the reliable
> servants of any ideology.

The first part of the sentence is a wonderful reason for teaching in all the ways we've been talking about. We want to see things in new ways; to see more, to see paintings, to see words, to see nature, to see people, to "see the world in a grain of sand." "The arts" is not a high-culture, exclusionist idea that shuts people out of Aladdin's cave: it's what crosses boundaries and brings us in there together.

But imagine the point of view of someone who has a particular ideology to sell or to enforce. First, you do not want people to be wasting their time reading, writing poetry, talking about philosophy, playing a saxophone up on the roof, when they should be at work, or learning better work skills. Life within an ideology is a serious business, and it doesn't allow time for what doesn't pay. Second, if your people do have to read some kind of stories or learn some kind of history, maybe you can control the particular books, the content, or what you will allow them to think about it, what questions they can ask. You certainly don't want them going off by themselves and picking any book they want; they might pick up a wrong idea. As for writing books (or blogs) themselves, that is out of the question, along with painting pictures that might disturb others or make them "see the world in a new way." Finally, you certainly don't want people wondering too much about what's going on outside of their own environment, especially considering other ways of thinking or living. No, overall it's better just to have them concentrate on the work you want them to do. You do allow them a few distractions and games, not the kind that make them think but enough to keep them busy.

Aldous Huxley imagined a similar *Brave New World* in the 1930's.[26] My high school English teacher thought Huxley was very relevant in the 1980's. We now seem even closer to a time when the arts and humanities are not locked up so much as blocked out. I live near two universities, the larger one well known for mathematics and technology, the smaller one focusing more on the arts. The second has recently announced a number of job cuts and the possible elimination of some programs. A spokesperson for the second university defended the cuts by saying that the first is financially stronger because it attracts a larger number of international students, and those students want computer science, not philosophy. Sad, but true.

> But the press and hurry of our times and the
> clamour for useful knowledge are driving
> classical culture out of the field...[27]

In contrast, Nussbaum quotes American philosopher Bronson Alcott (Louisa May Alcott's father), who dreamed of an education that opens out of the soul; we might also say, opens out the soul. Nussbaum calls it a "culture of creative innovation." It makes us grow, and makes our world bigger, more awesome...or, in another sense, smaller, more connected. To reverse Charlotte Mason's criticism, those educated in this way should have plenty of "initiative, the power of reflection and the sort of moral imagination that enables you to 'put yourself in his place.'"

The Way to Get There

Not for Profit says that citizens of a "humane, people-sensitive democracy" should be able to "think well about political issues": not necessarily understand everything, but be able to consider them.

> No nation can ever be great and hold a
> proud place among the nations of the world
> unless the men and women who are its
> citizens understand what their citizenship is,
> what it means to themselves and to their
> State, and try to live it out worthily. Its

citizens are a nation's real strength: their
personal quality is what counts in the
struggle of life. (F.R. Worts, *Citizenship*) [28]

Therefore, we need to teach a certain amount of civics and current events, all through the school years. At our house, my husband is the news-watcher (particularly of science news), so we often begin our school mornings with Dad's World Report.

But in the *Parents' Review* article discussed in the chapter on mathematics, Mary Everest Boole pointed out that it is not always the civics lessons that may affect our decisions later in life.

A politician might be saved from many an
error, by a picture cropping up at the right
moment to the surface of his thoughts: his
mother proposing to distribute the future
flowers by cutting the bulb into bits, or
asking him to find out by the multiplication-
table how much more mischief two boys can
do together than either would be likely to
invent alone.[29]

We need to build up the pictures, wherever they come from, and to allow time and space for reflection on them.

Chapter 10: Remaining Human

> Also, it is only a sense of the greatness of
> the poorest human soul that will awaken in
> us the passionate brotherhood which should
> help each of us to do our little share of the
> saving of the world...[1]

In high school French class, we read *Larmes de Silence (Tears of Silence)*, by Canadian philosopher and theologian Jean Vanier. It is a book of poetry about loneliness, hope, love, and the human family.[2] At the time I thought it was profound; later I was inclined to think my response was just teenage idealism, on the same level as teddy-bear posters and campfire songs. But I've gone back to believing that Vanier's thoughts are profound—and right. The effects of disconnection, if anything, have gotten worse in the half century since it was published. If education is the science of relations, alienation is the utter failure of education.

In his more recent book *Becoming Human*, Vanier says that

> Human beings need to be encouraged to
> make choices, and to become responsible
> for their own lives and for the lives of
> others. In order to make such choices, we
> need to reflect and to seek truth and
> meaning...to work, without fear, towards
> greater openness, greater understanding, and
> a greater love of others.[3]

Making choices, accepting responsibility? Charlotte Mason said the same thing: that the function of the Will is to choose, and that character means understanding responsibility. How is the Will enabled to make choices that are not only morally right, but compassionate and people-supporting?

Jean Vanier asks how we can

> orient the development of the individual
> towards works of justice, the struggle for
> peace, and helping others to develop their
> gifts and find their place in society?

This should speak strongly to those who teach, disciple, or counsel others; to educators, pastors, and parents; even to business leaders and administrators. The word "orient" implies focus, rather than force. Teachers and leaders can show sympathy and spread the feast; but it is the individual person who grows, who learns, and who is finally able to work towards peace and justice, helping others to find their belonging places.

Look at Charlotte Mason's last two principles:

> 19. Therefore, children should be taught, as
> they become mature enough to understand
> such teaching, that the chief responsibility
> which rests on them as persons is the
> acceptance or rejection of ideas. To help
> them in this choice we give them principles
> of conduct, and a wide range of the
> knowledge fitted to them. These principles
> should save children from some of the loose
> thinking and heedless action which cause
> most of us to live at a lower level than we
> need.

> 20. We allow no separation to grow up
> between the intellectual and "spiritual" life
> of children, but teach them that the Divine
> Spirit has constant access to their spirits, and
> is their Continual Helper in all the interests,
> duties and joys of life.

Truth and meaning in life come from the principles that people act on (because a principle does you no good if you just think about it). They are rooted in a particular rich knowledge-soil:

> ...[children establish] relations with places far
> and near, with the wide universe, with the
> past of history, with the social economics of
> the present, with the earth they live on and
> all its delightful progeny of beast and bird,
> plant and tree; with the sweet human
> affinities they entered into at birth; with
> their own country and other countries, and,
> above all, with that most sublime of human
> relationships—their relation to God.[4]

Skill in arithmetic, beautiful embroidery and music lessons won't get us there, no matter how nicely those subjects fill up a school day. Vocational training and technical skill are also empty by themselves. We need to spend a great deal of our time asking thinking questions. What's out there in the world and what are we doing about it? How does what people did long ago affect what we do now, and what our grandchildren will do tomorrow? If this is our Father's world, how do we acquire "listening ears?"

A few years ago, we were reading George MacDonald's fantasy novel *The Princess and Curdie*, which is the sequel to *The Princess and the Goblin*.[5] Curdie, the young hero of the first book, has now grown into a rather blasé teenager. He seems to have lost his imagination and bravery, and is living just for his daily drudge in the mines.

One day he shoots a pigeon near the castle where his friend Princess Irene used to live. As he does this, something seems to rattle him awake. When Curdie realizes that the bird isn't quite dead, the same something tells him to go to the castle and ask for help from Irene's mysterious "great-great-grandmother," whom he's actually never seen but who lives in the tower and seems to be connected with the birds. He struggles up the tower stairs, and is startled when she calls him in, by name. She forgives him for harming the bird, and gives him some advice and warnings. And the story goes on from there.

Later that same day I read a chapter of *The Call*, by Os Guinness. He describes some letters written in prison by Václav Havel.

> It is only by responding and growing responsible, Havel argues, that one "stands on one's own two feet." He then asserts what all his thinking has led him to: "I would say that responsibility for oneself is a knife we use to carve our own inimitable features in the panorama of Being; it is the pen with which we write into the history of Being that story of the fresh creation of the world that each new human existence always is."

Guinness again quotes Havel's letter:

> "someone eternal, who through himself makes me eternal as well...someone to whom I relate entirely and for whom, ultimately, I would do everything. At the same time, the 'someone' addresses me directly and personally."[6]

Yes, that's it, I thought, what Curdie had lost and what he seems to find again by visiting the grandmother: responsibility. There is a hidden meaning in that word: it also means "response-a-bility." And there's something more here: what Princess Irene's grandmother restores to Curdie is not just a grim reminder of duty and responsibility, but satisfaction, joy in living, what the Gospel of John calls abundance. It is not selfish to want to be truly happy, if our happiness comes from the right place and is directed at the right objects. Charlotte Mason said that it is our duty (and our pleasure!) to put that pursuit of true happiness into the hands of the children.

Going to the Source

> To use "good books," by way of a spiritual stimulus [*i.e. occasionally or at random*], deadens

in the end the healthy appetite for
truth...their tendency is to magnify ourselves
and our occasions, while they create in us
little or no desire for the best knowledge. It
is probable that even our lame efforts at
reading with understanding are more
profitable than the best instruction. The
preparedness we need is of the mind and
heart; we must...wait upon God as the
thirsty earth waits for rain.[7]

What awakens our spiritual minds?

If Curdie had only thought about visiting the tower, and imagined that he was forgiven, would it have been true? Or did he need to literally climb all those steps?

Charlotte Mason warned here about looking for "the best knowledge" in the wrong places, as well as the hazards of searching only when we feel like it.. Do helpful books and guides put the focus on our own selves and problems? Do they point us towards the best sources of truth, in this case the Bible? Or do they leave us pacified but not satisfied, with a false belief that we were actually there and performed the act of knowledge for ourselves?

To know him is life, and is the whole of
life...[8]

Sometimes the best thing to do is just read. But that also means effort, and putting our efforts in the right direction. It means persisting at building good habits, when our lazier side would prefer not to struggle. It means hard choices, in our teaching and in our personal lives. But it also means the joy of knowing that we have answered the one who calls us.

(Is it surprising that Charlotte Mason said more or less the same thing about science? "We can cover a mere inch of the field of Science, it is true; but the attitude of mind we get *in our own little bit of work* helps us to the understanding of what is being done elsewhere...") [9]

If You Feel Like Giving Up

Let us not put this sort of knowledge away
from us as too troublesome and as making
us too responsible. We have simply to know
in the first place; and are not bound to be
labouring all the time to feed imagination,
exercise reason, instruct conscience, and the
rest. In this sphere of self-knowledge, as in
so much else, set things going, and they
go;— "Begin it, and the thing will be
completed." [10]

In The End

"It is good to have been young in youth and, as years go on, to grow older... to travel deliberately through one's ages is to get the heart out of a liberal education. Times change, opinions vary to their opposite...and what can be more encouraging than to find the friend who was welcome at one age, still welcome at another? Our affections and beliefs are wiser than we; the best that is in us is better than we can understand; for it is grounded beyond experience, and guides us, blindfold but safe, from one age on to another." Robert Louis Stevenson[1]

So from here, where to? What to?

Our family is just weeks away from the end of homeschooling. Our oldest has a Bachelor of Science degree, a job, and an apartment; our second is graduating from high school; and our youngest will be bussing off to ninth grade come fall. I have given away or sold a large number of things that once defined us as homeschoolers and "Amblesiders": math manipulatives, printouts from *Viking Tales*, our copy of *Parables from Nature*. But we still have quite a bit, books that I think our high-schooler might need over the next few years, and things from the younger years that we insist on keeping, like the vinyl jump-on number line. We acquired that one quite early on in a yard-saled box of school treasures, along with a Bible and a set of *Little House* books. There is a lot of history in that number line. And in the hundred chart with poster-board discs that a first-grader carefully helped label. And in the paper dolls that the girls made to go with Marshall's history of England.

Many longtime homeschoolers have cultivated creative and frugal or low-tech homeschooling methods; and yet it's not even our children, necessarily, who most need that creativity. Using a deck of cards to teach math skills is a common example: you count the spots, you teach the numerals, you play variations on War. Don't most people have cards around the house, or pencils and paper, or dice? But to others, a deck of cards is just a deck of cards. The materials may be there, but the motivation and the knowledge to use them are not.[2]

Around the time that our oldest was in preschool, I met a young woman at the corner store. She had a little boy with her about my daughter's age, so I asked her if she knew about the parent-and-child programs at the community centre. She just looked at me without much interest and said, "He'd rather play in the toilet." Maybe she was joking; I've never been sure.

What *is* Charlotte Mason?

If there is anything I feel apologetic about in Charlotte Mason, it's that, often, homeschoolers have appropriated her ideas, made them our own, and turned Charlotte Mason into...well, *Charlotte Mason*. Something that takes us an hour to explain (including the necessary biographical details) and causes people to wonder (as one person asked hopefully), "Are there any *other* ways to homeschool?"

However... there are two points, two big ones anyway, that can be missed in our explanations. One is that Charlotte Mason headed the Parents' National Educational Union, which was a nation-wide, later a worldwide, group. In other words, it was not just Charlotte Mason and her best and closest friends; this was a large iron-sharpening-iron community. You can call her the inspiration, the head, even the heart behind this educational movement; but she didn't do it alone. It is good to introduce people to Charlotte Mason, but it doesn't always have to start with biographical details.

The second point is this: there is a need in the world for the wisdom-made-practical that we have benefited from ourselves, even if it's not labelled "C.M." or packaged in the way we expect. Susan Schaeffer Macaulay includes a description in *For the Children's Sake* of an arrangement where young girls (probably those who would be labelled at-risk) came to someone's house together, learned homemaking skills, and had discussion times over cups of coffee.

They might not have been interested in nature walks, but they did have ideas and questions. We need more people who can create safe, friendly spaces.

We need more English-as-a-second-language volunteers who marvel at the world coming to their doors. Literacy tutors as well.

We need more scientists and mathematicians who approach their work with a sense of awe. We definitely need more naturalists who are curious about local rocks, plants, animals, stargazing, and can share their interests. I just came across this quote from philosopher Josef Pieper:

> The one who wonders is one who sets out
> on a journey, and this journey goes along
> with the wonder: not only that he stops
> short for a moment, and is silent, but also
> that he persists in searching.[3]

We need more homeschool parents who will take on producing adaptations of Shakespeare plays, or of good books. Maybe over *large* cups of coffee.

We need more childcare providers and eldercare providers who understand beauty, compassion, imagination.

The world may not need (or think it needs) more "C.M." It may not want more homeschooling. However, it does need more magnanimity, more imagination, more humanness, more wonder. If that is what we're able to give our own children, that's good. But if we could find a way to pass it on even further...wouldn't that be amazing?

> What a reason have we here for doing
> whatever in us lies towards giving every
> person in the world the chance of being all
> that he came into the world provided and
> intended to be!....To know that we must
> order our thoughts; that we can do so; and
> how and when to interfere with the career of
> these same thoughts, is not the whole, but, I
> believe, it is half, the battle.[4]

Appendix: Charlotte Mason's 20 Principles

1. Children are born *persons*.

2. They are not born either good or bad, but with possibilities for good and for evil.

3. The principles of authority on the one hand, and of obedience on the other, are natural, necessary and fundamental; but—

4. These principles are limited by the respect due to the personality of children, which must not be encroached upon whether by the direct use of fear or love, suggestion or influence, or by undue play upon any one natural desire.

5. Therefore, we are limited to three educational instruments—the atmosphere of environment, the discipline of habit, and the presentation of living ideas. The P.N.E.U. Motto is: "Education is an atmosphere, a discipline, and a life."

6. When we say that "*education is an atmosphere*," we do not mean that a child should be isolated in what may be called a 'child-environment' especially adapted and prepared, but that we should take into account the educational value of his natural home atmosphere, both as regards persons and things, and should let him live freely among his proper conditions. It stultifies a child to bring down his world to the 'child's' level.

7. By "*education is a discipline*," we mean the discipline of habits, formed definitely and thoughtfully, whether habits of mind or body. Physiologists tell us of the adaptation of brain structures to habitual lines of thought, i.e., to our habits.

8. In saying that "*education is a life*," the need of intellectual and moral as well as of physical sustenance is implied. The mind feeds on ideas, and therefore children should have a generous curriculum.

9. We hold that the child's mind is no mere *sac* to hold ideas; but is rather, if the figure may be allowed, a spiritual *organism*, with an appetite for all knowledge. This is its proper diet, with which it is prepared to deal; and which it can digest and assimilate as the body does foodstuffs.

10. Such a doctrine as e.g. the Herbartian, that the mind is a receptacle, lays the stress of education (the preparation of knowledge in enticing morsels duly ordered) upon the teacher. Children taught on this principle are in danger of receiving much teaching with little knowledge; and the teacher's axiom is, "what a child learns matters less than how he learns it."

11. But we, believing that the normal child has powers of mind which fit him to deal with all knowledge proper to him, give him a full and generous curriculum; taking care only that all knowledge offered him is vital, that is, that facts are not presented without their informing ideas. Out of this conception comes our principle that,—

12. *"Education is the Science of Relations"*; that is, that a child has natural relations with a vast number of things and thoughts: so we train him upon physical exercises, nature lore, handicrafts, science and art, and upon *many living books*, for we know that our business is not to teach him all about anything, but to help him to make valid as many as may be of— *"Those first-born affinities / That fit our new existence to existing things."*

13. In devising a SYLLABUS for a normal child, of whatever social class, three points must be considered:

   a. He requires *much* knowledge, for the mind needs sufficient food as much as does the body.

   b. The knowledge should be various, for sameness in mental diet does not create appetite (i.e., curiosity)

   c. Knowledge should be communicated in well-chosen language, because his attention responds naturally to what is conveyed in literary form.

14. As knowledge is not assimilated until it is reproduced, children should 'tell back' after a single reading or hearing: or should write on some part of what they have read.

15. A *single reading* is insisted on, because children have naturally great power of attention; but this force is dissipated by the re-reading of passages, and also, by questioning, summarising. and the like.

   a. Acting upon these and some other points in the behaviour of mind, we find that *the educability of children is enormously greater than has hitherto been supposed*, and is but little dependent on such circumstances as heredity and environment.

b. Nor is the accuracy of this statement limited to clever children or to children of the educated classes: thousands of children in Elementary Schools respond freely to this method, which is based on the *behaviour of mind*.

16. There are two guides to moral and intellectual self-management to offer to children, which we may call 'the way of the will' and 'the way of the reason.'

17. *The way of the will*: Children should be taught, (a) to distinguish between 'I want' and 'I will.' (b) That the way to will effectively is to turn our thoughts from that which we desire but do not will. (c) That the best way to turn our thoughts is to think of or do some quite different thing, entertaining or interesting. (d) That after a little rest in this way, the will returns to its work with new vigour....

18. *The way of reason*: We teach children, too, not to 'lean (too confidently) to their own understanding'; because the function of reason is to give logical demonstration (a) of mathematical truth, (b) of an initial idea, accepted by the will. In the former case, reason is, practically, an infallible guide, but in the latter, it is not always a safe one; for, whether that idea be right or wrong, reason will confirm it by irrefragable proofs.

19. Therefore, children should be taught, as they become mature enough to understand such teaching, that the chief responsibility which rests on them as *persons* is the acceptance or rejection of ideas. To help them in this choice we give them principles of conduct, and a wide range of the knowledge fitted to them. These principles should save children from some of the loose thinking and heedless action which cause most of us to live at a lower level than we need.

20. We allow no separation to grow up between the intellectual and 'spiritual' life of children, but teach them that the Divine Spirit has constant access to their spirits, and is their Continual Helper in all the interests, duties and joys of life.

Notes

BEGINNINGS

1. Susan Schaeffer Macaulay, *For the Children's Sake* (Crossway, 1984).

2. *Whatever Happened to the Human Race?* (1979). A Christian response to abortion, euthanasia, and infanticide, narrated by Francis Schaeffer and former Surgeon General Dr. C. Everett Koop; the film series was released with a book by the same title.

3. Susan Schaeffer Macaulay, *For the Family's Sake* (Crossway, 1999).

4. Charlotte Mason's six volumes on education are *Home Education, Parents and Children, School Education, Ourselves, Formation of Character,* and *(Towards) A Philosophy of Education.* (Wheaton, IL: Tyndale House Publishers, Inc., 1989)

5. AmblesideOnline is a curriculum guide and booklist designed to follow Charlotte Mason's methods of homeschooling. http://www.amblesideonline.org

CHAPTER ONE

1. *Philosophy of Education,* p.281.

2. Peg Bracken, *The I Hate to Cookbook* (Fawcett Publications, 1960).

3. *Parents and Children,* "Preface to 3rd Edition."

4. Don Aslett's books include *Do I Dust Or Vacuum First?* (Writers Digest Books, 1982)

5. *Philosophy of Education,* p. 89-90

6.   *Philosophy of Education*, p.46.

7.   *Philosophy of Education*, p.48.

8.   *Formation of Character*, p.142.

9.   Jean-Jacques Rousseau (1712–1778) was a philosopher of the 18th century. His novel *Emile, or On Education*, contains his theories about childhood.

10.   *Parents and Children*, p.32.

CHAPTER TWO

1.   *Ourselves*, Book II, p.133.

2.   *Ourselves*, Book II, pp.141-142.

3.   Lucius Mestrius Plutarchus (Plutarch) was a Greek writer (but a Roman citizen), who lived from 46-120 AD. He is best known for his *Lives of the Noble Greeks and Romans*.

4.   *Home Education*, p.98.

5.   *Home Education*, p.105.

6.   *Home Education*, p.109.

7.   David V. Hicks, *Norms & Nobility* (Lanham, MD: University Press of America, 1999).

8.   Martha C. Nussbaum, *Not for Profit: Why Democracy Needs the Humanities* (Princeton, NJ: Princeton UP, 2010).

9.   *The great didactic of John Amos Comenius*, by M.W. Keatinge, B.A. (Adam & Charles Black, 1896), p. 224. https://archive.org/details/greatdidacticofj00come

10.   Mrs. [Emily] Ward, "'Grit,' Or Raising and Educating our Children," *The Parents' Review*, 2 (1891/92): 49, AmblesideOnline. https://www.amblesideonline.org/PR/PR02p049Grit.shtml. *The Parents' Review* was first edited by Charlotte Mason. It included articles, news and notes from what was originally called the

Parents' Review School, then the Parents' Union School, and finally PNEU (Parents' National Educational Union).

11. Sandy Rusby Bell, "Wonder and Admiration: Elementary Science and Nature Study," at K-W Christian Home Educators' Conference, Kitchener, Ontario, March 2015.

12. *The Pond on My Windowsill: the story of a freshwater aquarium*, by Christopher Reynolds (HarperCollins Distribution Services, 1969).

13. Miss M. Ambler, "'Plutarch's Lives' as Affording Some Education as a Citizen," *The Parents' Review*, 12 (1901): 521-527, AmblesideOnline.https://www.amblesideonline.org/PR/PR12p5 21PlutarchsLives.shtml

14. Beatrix Potter, *The Tale of Jemima Puddle-Duck* (Frederick Warne & Co., 1908).

15. *Philosophy of Education*, p.130.

16. "New every morning is the love," by John Keble, from "Morning" in *The Christian Year*, 1827. http://www.hymntime.com/tch/htm/n/e/w/newevery.htm

17. *Ourselves*, Book II, p.128.

18. *Home Education*, p.100.

LOST TREASURES #1

1. Richard J. Maybury, *Uncle Eric Talks About Personal, Career, and Financial Security (An Uncle Eric Book)* (Bluestocking Press, 1994).

CHAPTER THREE

2. Charlotte Mason, "Preface to the Home Education Series," found at the beginning of each volume.

3. S. De Brath, "A Rational Lesson." Part One, *The Parents' Review*, 8 (1897): 119-125, AmblesideOnline. https://www.amblesideonline.org/PR/PR08p119RationalLesson. shtml

4.   Part Two, *The Parents' Review*, 8 (1897): 298-306,
        AmblesideOnline.
        http://www.amblesideonline.org/PR/PR08p298RationalLesson.s
        html

5.   *Parents and Children*, page 231.

6.   *Philosophy of Education*, pp. 96-97.

7.   *Understood Betsy*, by Dorothy Canfield (Fisher) (New York:
        Grosset & Dunlap, 1917).
        https://archive.org/details/understoodbetsy0fishe

8.   "A Rational Lesson" (note 2).

9.   *Parents and Children*, p.231.

10.   Frederick Buechner, *The Alphabet of Grace* (Harper & Row, 1970)

11.   *Philosophy of Education*, pp.290-291.

12.   *Home Education*, p.151.

13.   *Ourselves*, Book I, p.61.

14.   *Philosophy of Education*, p.143.

15.   Charles Kingsley, *Madam How and Lady Why, or, First Lessons in
        Earth Lore for Children*. (Macmillan & Co, 1885 (online edition)).
        https://archive.org/details/madamhowandlady00kinggoog

16.   *Philosophy of Education*, p.3.

17.   *School Education*, pp.178-179.

18.   "Notes of Lessons," *The Parents' Review*, 15 (1904): 67-68,
        AmblesideOnline.
        http://www.amblesideonline.org/PR/PR15p067NotesofLessons.
        shtml

19.   Mortimer J. Adler and Charles Van Doren, *How to Read a Book*
        (Revised and Updated Edition). (Simon and Schuster, 1972).

CHAPTER FOUR

1. *Philosophy of Education*, p.26.

2. Elizabeth Enright, *The Four-Story Mistake* (Farrar & Rinehart, 1942).

3. *Philosophy of Education*, p.29-30.

4. Miss M. Ambler, "'Plutarch's Lives' as Affording Some Education as a Citizen." See Chapter 2, Note 13.

5. *Ourselves*, Book I, p.78.

6. *School Education*, p. 99.

7. S. De Brath, "A Rational Lesson." See Chapter 3, Note 2.

8. John Adams, *Herbartian Psychology Applied to Education* (D.C. Heath and Company, 1898/9). https://archive.org/details/herbartianpsych00adamgoog

9. *Philosophy of Education*, p.130.

10. Mrs.[Emily Mary] Dowson, "The Discipline and Organization of the Mind," *The Parents' Review*, 11 (1900): 83-92, AmblesideOnline. https://www.amblesideonline.org/PR/PR11p083DisciplineofMind.shtml

11. *Philosophy of Education*, p.43.

12. Mrs. Dowson (see Note 10).

13. C.S. Lewis, *The Voyage of the Dawn Treader* (Geoffrey Bles, 1952).

14. *Philosophy of Education*, p.26.

15. St. Aurelius Augustine (author), George G. Leckie (translator), *Concerning the Teacher and On the Immortality of the Soul* (Appleton, 1938).

16. S. De Brath, "A Rational Lesson, Part 2," *The Parents' Review* 8 (1897):298-306. Charlotte Mason Digital Archive. Redeemer

University College,
http://charlottemason.redeemer.ca/ParentsReview/PRv8PDFs/n5/p287-292PRv8n5.pdf

17. See 16.

18. Mrs. Dowson (see Note 10).

19. *Philosophy of Education*, p.59.

20. Examples of original school programmes can be seen on the AmblesideOnline website, www.amblesideonline.org .

21. *School Education*, p.178.

22. Isaac Asimov, *How Did We Find Out About Electricity?* (Walker & Co., 1973).

23. *School Education*, p.225.

24. *Home Education*, p.266.

25. Edward S. Holden, *The Sciences* (The Athaeneum Press, 1902). http://home.comcast.net/~rlaurio/TheSciences00.html

26. Mabel Dunham, *The Trail of the Conestoga* (McClelland and Stewart, 1942).

27. Cuisenaire Rods are a set of coloured number rods created by Belgian primary school teacher Georges Cuisenaire (1891-1975). http://www.cuisenaire.co.uk/

28. *Parents and Children*, p.200.

CHAPTER FIVE

1. *Ourselves*, Book I, page 85.

2. Louisa May Alcott, *Eight Cousins* (Roberts Bros, Boston, 1875).

3. One example is *Noah's Children: Restoring the Ecology of Childhood*, by Sara Stein (North Point Press, 2001).

4. Peter Andrey Smith. "Dusty Dozing." *Scientific American*. Apr. 2015: 26. Print.

5.   *Parents and Children*, p.168.

6.   Laura Ingalls Wilder, *Little House in the Big Woods* (Harper & Brothers, 1953).

7.   Phyllis McGinley, *The Plain Princess* (J. B. Lippincott Company, 1945).

8.   Ruth T. Stamper, "Rebuke," *Christian Living: A Magazine for Home and Community*, 12 (1965).

9.   *Parents and Children*, p.18.

10.   *Home Education*, p.131.

11.   *Philosophy of Education*, p. 131.

12.   "The Cage." *Foyle's War*. ITV. 31 March 2013 (UK). Television.

CHAPTER SIX

1.   H.E. Marshall, *English Literature for Boys and Girls* (London, Edinburgh. T.E. & E.C. Jack, Ltd., 1909). https://archive.org/details/englishliteratur00mars

2.   *Philosophy of Education*, p.302.

3.   Sir Walter Scott, *Ivanhoe* (A. Constable, 1820).

4.   C.S. Lewis, *The Voyage of the Dawn Treader*. See Chapter 4, Note 13.

5.   Feodor Dostoevsky, *Notes from Underground* (Serialized in *Epoch*, January–April 1864. First published in English 1918.)

6.   *Home Education*, p. 216.

7.   "Notes of Lessons," *The Parents' Review* 17 (1906): 468. Retrieved from the "Archipelago" blog, May 11, 2015. http://archipelago7.blogspot.ca/2015/04/from-parents-review-early-reading-lesson.html The lesson is based on a page in *The Happy Reader, Part II: Short-Vowel Stories, Rhymes and Plays*, by E.L. Young (London: Simpkin, Marshall, Hamilton, Kent & Co., approx. 1893). Special thanks to Sonya Shafer of Simply Charlotte Mason for verifying this information.

8.   D. Brownell, "Notes of Lessons," *The Parents' Review* 15 (1904): 310. Retrieved from the "Archipelago" blog, May 11, 2015. http://archipelago7.blogspot.ca/2015/04/another-early-reading-lesson-parents.html

9.   "A Friend in the Garden,"in *The Project Gutenberg E-Book of Verses for Children*, by Juliana Horatia Ewing (Project Gutenberg, September 12, 2005). http://www.gutenberg.org/files/16686/16686-h/16686-h.htm

10.   The Martha series begins with *Little House in the Highlands*, by Melissa Wiley (HarperTrophy 1999).

11.   *Home Education*, p. 231.

12.   *Philosophy of Education*, p.290-291.

13.   *Philosophy of Education*, p.291.

14.   Dallas Lore Sharp, *Summer* (Houghton Mifflin, 1914). https://archive.org/details/summersharpdalla00sharrich.

15.   Russell Hoban, *Bread and Jam for Frances* (Harper & Row, 1964).

16.   Mortimer J. Adler, *How to Read a Book*. See Chapter 3, Note 17.

17.   James Baldwin, *Fifty Famous Stories Retold* (American Book Company, 1896). https://archive.org/details/fiftyfamousstor00baldgoog

18.   Pierre Grimal, *Stories of Alexander the Great*. Edited and translated from the French by Barbara Whelpton. (Burke Publishing Company 1965).

19.   Plato, *Meno*. For a discussion of this idea, see Louis Markos, "Plato's Big Mistake," on "The Imaginative Conservative" blog. http://www.theimaginativeconservative.org/2013/10/platos-big-mistake-knowledge-is-virtue.html. Retrieved 4/25/15.

20.   *Parents and Children*, p.271.

21.   *School Education*, p.342-343; my adaptation.

22. H.E. Marshall, *English Literature for Boys and Girls*; see Note 1.

23. *Philosophy of Education*, p.183.

24. Northrop Frye, *The Educated Imagination* (Canadian Broadcasting Corporation, 1963), p. 2.

25. D. Stevenson, M.A., "The Teaching of Literature," *The Parents' Review*, 11 (1900): 102-108, AmblesideOnline. https://www.amblesideonline.org/PR/PR11p102TeachingLiterat ure.shtml

26. S. De Brath, "A Rational Lesson." See Chapter 3, Note 2.

27. "Chevy Chase," on http://www.contemplator.com.

CHAPTER SEVEN

1. Charlotte Mason ("The Editor"), "The Parents' Review School," *The Parents' Review*, 2 (1891/92): 308-317, AmblesideOnline. http://www.amblesideonline.org/PR/PR02p308PRSchool.shtml

2. Mrs. [Emily] Ward, "'Grit,' Or Raising and Educating our Children." See Chapter 2, Note 10.

3. *Formation of Character*, p. 95.

4. *Parents and Children*, p.17.

5. Mrs. Ward; see Chapter 2, Note 10.

6. Mrs.Edward Sieveking, "Early Tendencies in the Child: How to Check Them or Develop," *The Parents' Review*, 14 (1903): 495-505, AmblesideOnline. https://www.amblesideonline.org/PR/PR14p495EarlyTendencie s.shtml

7. St. Thomas Aquinas, *Summa Theologica*.

8. *Meet the Malones*, by Lenora Mattingly Weber (New York: Thomas Y. Crowell Co., 1943/Image Cascade Publishing, 1999).

CHAPTER EIGHT

1.   Mary Everest Boole, "Nursery Examples of Fractions," *Parents' Review*, 8 (1897): 76-82, AmblesideOnline. https://www.amblesideonline.org/PR/PR08p076NurseryFractions.shtml

2.   See Chapter 2, Note 10.

3.   Harold Jacobs, *Mathematics: A Human Endeavor*, 3rd Edition (W.H. Freeman and Company, 1994).

4.   Mary Everest Boole, "Home Algebra and Geometry," *Parents' Review*, 3 (1892/3): 854-857, AmblesideOnline. https://www.amblesideonline.org/PR/PR04p854HomeAlgebra.shtml

5.   Mary Everest Boole, "Home Arithmetic," *The Parents' Review*, 4 (1893/4):649-654, AmblesideOnline. https://www.amblesideonline.org/PR/PR04p649HomeArithmetic.shtml

LOST TREASURES #3

1.   Louisa May Alcott, *Jack and Jill: A Village Story* (Roberts Brothers, 1880). https://archive.org/details/jackandjillavil00alcogoog

2.   *Ourselves*, Book I, p. 96.

CHAPTER NINE

1.   Plutarch, "Life of Dion." http://www.amblesideonline.org/PlDion.shtml

2.   Plutarch, "Life of Publicola." https://archive.org/details/livesenglishedb01plut

3.   AmblesideOnline provides study notes for some of Plutarch's Lives. http://www.amblesideonline.org/PlutarchSch.shtml

4.   Plutarch, "Life of Publicola."

5.   Ralph Waldo Emerson, "Plutarch." *The Complete Works, Vol. X.*

Lectures and Biographical Sketches (1904).
http://www.bartleby.com/90/1011.html

6.   *Parents and Children*, pp.231-232.

7.   Nathaniel Hawthorne, *Tanglewood Tales* (1853).

8.   *Home Education*, p.286.

9.   Plutarch, "Life of Timoleon."
     http://www.amblesideonline.org/PlTimoleon.shtml

10. *In Memoriam*, Parents' National Educational Union, 1923.
     http://www.amblesideonline.org/CM/InMemoriam.html

11. Miss M. Ambler, "'Plutarch's Lives' as Affording Some Education
     as a Citizen." See Chapter 2, Note 13.

12. F.R. Worts, *Citizenship, its meaning, privileges and duties* (Hodder and
     Stoughton, 1919).
     https://archive.org/details/citizenshipitsme00wort

13. Plutarch, "Life of Dion."

14. C.S. Lewis, *The Last Battle* (The Bodley Head, 1956).

15. *Home Education*, p. 278.

16. *It's a Wonderful Life*. Dir. Frank Capra. Liberty Films, 1946.

17. "The Label Doesn't Tell the Whole Story, "Canadian Fair Trade
     Network website. http://cftn.ca/campaigns/label-doesnt-tell-
     whole-story Retrieved April 28, 2015.

18. "Ten Thousand Villages' mission is to create opportunities for
     artisans in developing countries to earn income by bringing their
     products and stories to our markets through long-term fair
     trading relationships." http://www.tenthousandvillages.com/

19. *Formation of Character*, p.206.

20. *Home Education*, p. 289.

21. *The Parents' Review* 15 (1904): 144-147. Retrieved from the
     "Archipelago" blog May 11,

2015. http://archipelago7.blogspot.ca/2015/04/notes-of-lessons-from-parents-review.html

22. *Ourselves*, Book II, p.98.

23. *Ourselves*, Book II, p.100.

24. Martha C. Nussbaum, *Not for Profit: Why Democracy Needs the Humanities* (Princeton University Press, 2010).

25. Utilitarianism: believing that a person's value is based on his or her usefulness to society; people are part of the collective or "machine."

26. Aldous Huxley, *Brave New World* (Chatto & Windus, 1932).

27. *Formation of Character*, p. 213.

28. See Note 12.

29. Mary Everest Boole, "Nursery Examples of Fractions." See Chapter 8, Note 1.

CHAPTER TEN

1. *Ourselves*, Book II, p.108.

2. Jean Vanier, *Tears of Silence* (House of Anansi Press; Reprint, 2014).

3. Jean Vanier, *Becoming Human* (House of Anansi Press, 1998).

4. *Philosophy of Education*, pp.72-73.

5. George MacDonald, *The Princess and the Goblin* (Strahan & Co., 1872). *The Princess and Curdie* (J.B. Lippincott & Co., 1883).

6. *The Call: Finding and Fulfilling the Central Purpose of Your Life*, by Os Guinness (Thomas Nelson, 2003).

7. *Ourselves*, Book II, p.84.

8. *Ourselves*, Book II, p.91.

9. *Ourselves*, Book II, page 101 (italics mine)

10.   *Ourselves*, Book II, p.108.

IN THE END

1.   Robert Louis Stevenson, *Virginibus Puerisque and Other Papers* (Chatto & Windus, 1887).
        https://archive.org/details/virginibuspueri01stev

2.   There are many books and websites with suggestions for math and other learning games. One we used was Peggy Kaye's *Games for Learning* (Farrar, Straus, & Giroux, 1991).

3.   Josef Pieper, *Leisure: The Basis of Culture.* New translation by Gerald Malsbary. (St. Augustine's Press, South Bend, Indiana, 1998)

4.   *Ourselves*, Book I, pp.79-80.

Books, Quoted and Useful

Bestvater, Laurie. 2013. *The Living Page: Keeping Notebooks with Charlotte Mason*. Underpinnings Press.

Frye, Northrop. 1963. *The Educated Imagination*. Canadian Broadcasting Corporation.

Glass, Karen. 2014. *Consider This: Charlotte Mason and the Classical Tradition*. Foreword by David V. Hicks.

Hicks, David V. 1999. *Norms and Nobility*. Lanham: MD: University Press of America.

Macaulay, Susan Schaeffer. 1994/2009. *For the Children's Sake*. Wheaton, Illinois: Crossway.

Macaulay, Susan Schaeffer. 1999. *For the Family's Sake*. Wheaton, Illinois: Crossway.

Mason, Charlotte M. 1886. *Home Education*. Reprint, with foreword by John Thorley. Wheaton, IL: Tyndale House, 1989.

Mason, Charlotte M. 1896. *Parents and Children*. Reprint, with foreword by John Thorley. Wheaton, IL: Tyndale House, 1989.

Mason, Charlotte M. 1904. *School Education.*. Reprint, with foreword by John Thorley. Wheaton, IL: Tyndale House, 1989.

Mason, Charlotte M. 1905. *Ourselves*. Reprint, with foreword by John Thorley. Wheaton, IL: Tyndale House, 1989.

Mason, Charlotte M. 1906. *Formation of Character*. Reprint, with foreword by John Thorley. Wheaton, IL: Tyndale House, 1989.

Mason, Charlotte M. 1925. *A Philosophy of Education*. Reprint, with foreword by John Thorley. Wheaton, IL: Tyndale House, 1989.

Nussbaum, Martha C. 2010. *Not for Profit: Why Democracy Needs the Humanities*. Princeton, NJ: Princeton UP.

Vanier, Jean. 1998. *Becoming Human*. Toronto: House of Anansi Press.

About the Author

Anne E. White (www.annewrites.ca) has shared her knowledge of Charlotte Mason's methods through magazine columns, online writing, and conference workshops. She is an Advisory member of AmblesideOnline, for which she writes an ongoing series of Plutarch study notes. The Whites homeschooled their three daughters for nineteen memorable years.

Made in the USA
Middletown, DE
12 August 2015